Joyce Appleby on *Thomas Jefferson*
Louis Auchincloss on *Theodore Roosevelt*
Jean H. Baker on *James Buchanan*
H. W. Brands on *Woodrow Wilson*
Alan Brinkley on *John F. Kennedy*
Douglas Brinkley on *Gerald R. Ford*
Josiah Bunting III on *Ulysses S. Grant*
James MacGregor Burns and Susan Dunn on *George Washington*
Charles W. Calhoun on *Benjamin Harrison*
Gail Collins on *William Henry Harrison*
Robert Dallek on *Harry S. Truman*
John W. Dean on *Warren G. Harding*
John Patrick Diggins on *John Adams*
Elizabeth Drew on *Richard M. Nixon*
John S. D. Eisenhower on *Zachary Taylor*
Annette Gordon-Reed on *Andrew Johnson*
Henry F. Graff on *Grover Cleveland*
David Greenberg on *Calvin Coolidge*
Gary Hart on *James Monroe*
Hendrik Hertzberg on *Jimmy Carter*
Roy Jenkins on *Franklin Delano Roosevelt*
Zachary Karabell on *Chester Alan Arthur*
Lewis H. Lapham on *William Howard Taft*
William E. Leuchtenburg on *Herbert Hoover*
Gary May on *John Tyler*
George S. McGovern on *Abraham Lincoln*
Timothy Naftali on *George Bush*
Charles Peters on *Lyndon B. Johnson*
Kevin Phillips on *William McKinley*
Robert V. Remini on *John Quincy Adams*
Ira Rutkow on *James A. Garfield*
John Seigenthaler on *James K. Polk*
Hans L. Trefousse on *Rutherford B. Hayes*
Tom Wicker on *Dwight D. Eisenhower*
Ted Widmer on *Martin Van Buren*
Sean Wilentz on *Andrew Jackson*
Garry Wills on *James Madison*

Calvin Coolidge

David Greenberg

Calvin Coolidge

THE AMERICAN PRESIDENTS

ARTHUR M. SCHLESINGER, JR., GENERAL EDITOR

Times Books

HENRY HOLT AND COMPANY, NEW YORK

Times Books
Henry Holt and Company, LLC
Publishers since 1866
175 Fifth Avenue
New York, New York 10010

Henry Holt® is a registered trademark
of Henry Holt and Company, LLC.

Library of Congress Cataloging-in-Publication Data
Greenberg, David, 1968–
    Calvin Coolidge / David Greenberg.
        p. cm.—(The American presidents)
    Includes bibliographical references and index.
    ISBN-13: 978-0-8050-6957-0
    ISBN-10: 0-8050-6957-7
    1. Coolidge, Calvin, 1872–1933.   2. Presidents—United States—Biography.
3. United States—Politics and government—1923–1929.   I. Title.

E792.G75 2006
973.91'5092—dc22
[B]   2006050113

First Edition 2007

Printed in the United States of America
1 3 5 7 9 10 8 6 4 2

To Leo

Contents

Editor's Note

―――――

THE AMERICAN PRESIDENCY

The president is the central player in the American political order. That would seem to contradict the intentions of the Founding Fathers. Remembering the horrid example of the British monarchy, they invented a separation of powers in order, as Justice Brandeis later put it, "to preclude the exercise of arbitrary power." Accordingly, they divided the government into three allegedly equal and coordinate branches—the executive, the legislative, and the judiciary.

But a system based on the tripartite separation of powers has an inherent tendency toward inertia and stalemate. One of the three branches must take the initiative if the system is to move. The executive branch alone is structurally capable of taking that initiative. The Founders must have sensed this when they accepted Alexander Hamilton's proposition in the Seventieth Federalist that "energy in the executive is a leading character in the definition of good government." They thus envisaged a strong president—but within an equally strong system of constitutional accountability. (The term *imperial presidency* arose in the 1970s to describe the situation when the balance between power and accountability is upset in favor of the executive.)

The American system of self-government thus comes to focus in the presidency—"the vital place of action in the system," as Woodrow Wilson put it. Henry Adams, himself the great-grandson and grandson of presidents as well as the most brilliant of American historians, said that the American president "resembles the commander of a ship at sea. He must have a helm to grasp, a course to steer, a port to seek." The men in the White House (thus far only men, alas) in steering their chosen courses have shaped our destiny as a nation.

Biography offers an easy education in American history, rendering the past more human, more vivid, more intimate, more accessible, more connected to ourselves. Biography reminds us that presidents are not supermen. They are human beings too, worrying about decisions, attending to wives and children, juggling balls in the air, and putting on their pants one leg at a time. Indeed, as Emerson contended, "There is properly no history; only biography."

Presidents serve us as inspirations, and they also serve us as warnings. They provide bad examples as well as good. The nation, the Supreme Court has said, has "no right to expect that it will always have wise and humane rulers, sincerely attached to the principles of the Constitution. Wicked men, ambitious of power, with hatred of liberty and contempt of law, may fill the place once occupied by Washington and Lincoln."

The men in the White House express the ideals and the values, the frailties and the flaws, of the voters who send them there. It is altogether natural that we should want to know more about the virtues and the vices of the fellows we have elected to govern us. As we know more about them, we will know more about ourselves. The French political philosopher Joseph de Maistre said, "Every nation has the government it deserves."

At the start of the twenty-first century, forty-two men have made it to the Oval Office. (George W. Bush is counted our forty-third president, because Grover Cleveland, who served nonconsecutive terms, is counted twice.) Of the parade of presidents, a dozen

or so lead the polls periodically conducted by historians and political scientists. What makes a great president?

Great presidents possess, or are possessed by, a vision of an ideal
America. Their passion, as they grasp the helm, is to set the ship of
state on the right course toward the port they seek. Great presidents also have a deep psychic connection with the needs, anxieties,
dreams of people. "I do not believe," said Wilson, "that any man can
lead who does not act . . . under the impulse of a profound sympathy with those whom he leads—a sympathy which is insight—an
insight which is of the heart rather than of the intellect."

"All of our great presidents," said Franklin D. Roosevelt, "were
leaders of thought at a time when certain ideas in the life of the
nation had to be clarified." So Washington incarnated the idea of
federal union, Jefferson and Jackson the idea of democracy, Lincoln
union and freedom, Cleveland rugged honesty. Theodore Roosevelt
and Wilson, said FDR, were both "moral leaders, each in his own
way and his own time, who used the presidency as a pulpit."

To succeed, presidents not only must have a port to seek but
they must convince Congress and the electorate that it is a port
worth seeking. Politics in a democracy is ultimately an educational
process, an adventure in persuasion and consent. Every president
stands in Theodore Roosevelt's bully pulpit.

The greatest presidents in the scholars' rankings, Washington,
Lincoln, and Franklin Roosevelt, were leaders who confronted and
overcame the republic's greatest crises. Crisis widens presidential
opportunities for bold and imaginative action. But it does not guarantee presidential greatness. The crisis of secession did not spur
Buchanan or the crisis of depression spur Hoover to creative leadership. Their inadequacies in the face of crisis allowed Lincoln and
the second Roosevelt to show the difference individuals make to
history. Still, even in the absence of first-order crisis, forceful and
persuasive presidents—Jefferson, Jackson, James K. Polk, Theodore
Roosevelt, Harry Truman, John F. Kennedy, Ronald Reagan, George
W. Bush—are able to impose their own priorities on the country.

The diverse drama of the presidency offers a fascinating set of tales. Biographies of American presidents constitute a chronicle of wisdom and folly, nobility and pettiness, courage and cunning, forthrightness and deceit, quarrel and consensus. The turmoil perennially swirling around the White House illuminates the heart of the American democracy.

It is the aim of the American Presidents series to present the grand panorama of our chief executives in volumes compact enough for the busy reader, lucid enough for the student, authoritative enough for the scholar. Each volume offers a distillation of character and career. I hope that these lives will give readers some understanding of the pitfalls and potentialities of the presidency and also of the responsibilities of citizenship. Truman's famous sign—"The buck stops here"—tells only half the story. Citizens cannot escape the ultimate responsibility. It is in the voting booth, not on the presidential desk, that the buck finally stops.

—Arthur M. Schlesinger, Jr.

Calvin Coolidge

Introduction

When Ronald Reagan was elected president of the United States in November 1980, he pledged to restore certain old-fashioned values to public life: patriotism and piety, hard work and thrift. To underscore the point, one of the first changes he made on entering the White House in January was to take down the portraits of Thomas Jefferson and Harry Truman in the Cabinet Room and put up those of Dwight Eisenhower and Calvin Coolidge.[1]

Reagan's choice of the genial, avuncular Eisenhower most Americans could understand, if not necessarily endorse. In contrast, the exaltation of Coolidge appeared, at best, idiosyncratic. President from 1923, when he acceded to the office upon the sudden death of Warren Harding, until 1929, when he retired after forswearing a second full term, Coolidge was enormously popular throughout his tenure—an icon of his era every bit as much as Charles Lindbergh, Babe Ruth, or Charlie Chaplin. Yet by 1981 the long-departed Yankee Republican figured only marginally in the history books and even less so in the nation's collective memory. Coolidge's popular reputation, such as it was, had hardened into a cartoon—one that endures today.

Coolidge has become the grim-faced "Silent Cal"—Theodore Roosevelt's daughter Alice made famous the judgment that he looked "as if he had been weaned on a pickle"—and a consummately passive president. "His ideal day," mocked his contemporary

H. L. Mencken, "is one on which nothing whatever happens." He is still remembered as he was seen by the "smart set" of the 1920s—intellectuals and writers like Mencken, Walter Lippmann, and William Allen White—who berated him as a mediocrity and a stooge of the business class. In popular culture, Coolidge survived not in weighty biographies but tucked away in novels such as Nathanael West's 1934 gem, *A Cool Million*, which parodies Coolidge as the former president Shagpoke Whipple, whose Horatio Alger–style platitudes, in the desperation of the Depression, curdle into fascism. With his nineteenth-century regard for individual integrity, esteem for business, and taste for small government, Coolidge has stood distant and indistinct across the chasm introduced into history by the New Deal and World War II.[2]

Yet to Ronald Reagan, who was a teenager during Coolidge's presidency, Silent Cal remained a hero, "one of our most underrated presidents." Throughout his two terms in office, Reagan perused Coolidge speeches and biographies; after his 1985 cancer surgery, Reagan was seen in his recovery room reading a book about Silent Cal. His staff brought to the White House the conservative writer Thomas Silver, whose 1982 book *Coolidge and the Historians* argued that liberal scholars had given Coolidge a bum rap. Reagan agreed. "I happen to be an admirer of Silent Cal and believe he has been badly treated by history," Reagan told a correspondent. "I've done considerable reading and researching of his presidency. He served his country well and accomplished much." More important, Reagan drew on Coolidge's homilies for his own statements, and in 1981, when he fired striking air traffic controllers, he took inspiration from Coolidge's tough line in 1919 against striking Boston policemen.[3]

Other Reaganites similarly found a model in the neglected president. *Wall Street Journal* editorialist Jude Wanniski, the apostle of supply-side economics, viewed Coolidge as an unsung prophet. The columnist Robert Novak ranked Coolidge as his second favorite American leader—after Reagan, of course—and the Republican consultant Roger Stone hosted annual celebrations of the former president on July 4, which happened to be Silent Cal's birthday. In

September 2006, the conservative Heritage Foundation hosted an evening entitled "Coolidge: A Life for Our Time," featuring a premiere screening of "the first film ever made of the personal and political life of Calvin Coolidge." Nonetheless, amid all the scholarly attention devoted of late to the founders of post–World War II conservatism, Coolidge and the avatars of the conservative prewar years have remained largely overlooked.[4]

Foremost among Coolidge's achievements, for Reagan and his followers, were the economic policies he pursued, which helped maintain a robust prosperity for his five and a half years in office— but also contributed to the crash and Great Depression that followed. Reagan remembered only the upside. "He cut the taxes four times," Reagan said in 1981 of Silent Cal. "We had probably the greatest growth and prosperity that we've ever known. And I have taken heed of that, because if he did nothing, maybe that's the answer [for] the federal government." Coolidge also succeeded in doing something that Reagan could not: he paid down the federal debt substantially—the last president to do so until Bill Clinton.[5]

To Reagan and his supporters, Coolidge represented an ideal. They shared with him not just a belief in small government but also its flip side: a faith in a mythic America in which hardworking, God-fearing neighbors buffered one another from hardship. Both men felt confident that private virtue could check the threat of moral decay brought on by modern changes. Where Reagan pined for the small towns of the 1920s, Coolidge waxed nostalgic for the nineteenth-century Vermont of his youth, a world of *McGuffey's Readers* and toil on the farm, Congregationalist churches and town meetings. Less a censorious Puritan than a pious man of sentimental faith, Coolidge shunned the era's new secularism as well as its resurgent fundamentalism; he saw religion as a source of virtue, not of division, oppression, or intellectual limitation.[6]

Business, likewise, was for him benign, not predatory. In the early decades of the twentieth century, Progressive Era reforms had countered some of the worst depredations of the unfettered capitalism of the Gilded Age. By the 1920s, a view was emerging that capitalists' new sense of social responsibility would preclude the need for aggressive federal intervention in the marketplace. Coolidge shared this view. A believer in the regnant economic orthodoxy of Say's Law—the notion, propounded by the French economist Jean-Baptiste Say, that supply creates its own demand—Coolidge held that industrial productivity, by generating prosperity, would serve the general good. Indeed, he equated the public interest not with some consensus brokered to satisfy competing social factions but with something close to the needs of industry itself. He wanted, as he once said, "to encourage business, not merely for its own sake but because that is the surest method of administering to the common good."[7]

Coolidge famously summarized this philosophy in his January 1925 declaration to the American Society of Newspaper Editors: "The chief business of America is business." Although sometimes caricatured as a sign of Coolidge's obeisance to corporations, the statement actually contained a more subtle though still pro-business message. No apologist for raw laissez-faire, Coolidge believed that public-spiritedness was needed to counter the corrupting temptations of the profit motive. He was reminding the editors that they had to remain high-minded if the commercially driven newspaper business was to benefit the public. "The chief ideal of the American people," he explained, "is idealism." And Coolidge's economic outlook was indeed idealistic.[8]

·   ·   ·

Besides sharing an idealized image of America, Ronald Reagan resembled Calvin Coolidge in another important sense. For all his paeans to an idyllic past, Reagan was decidedly forward-looking in several respects: his delight in a consumer society, his use of communications media to advance his goals, and his conception of presidential leadership. The same was true of Coolidge.

Although the fires of political progressivism cooled in the 1920s, social change and modernization continued. The sociologists Robert and Helen Lynd called the decade "one of the eras of greatest rapidity in change in the history of human institutions." America was plunging headlong into modernity, with its whirligig of jazz and speakeasies, Model Ts and skyscrapers, movies and radios, liberated women and the "New Negro." The consumer economy was enshrining a habit of self-definition based on pleasure, leisure, and personal choice, displacing an older ethic of ascetic living and pride in one's craft. Sitting aloof from it all in Washington, with his woolen suits, Victorian mores, and disapproving grimace, the dour Coolidge seemed to many a world apart. "We were smack in the middle of the Roaring Twenties, with hip flasks, joy rides, and bathtub gin parties setting the social standards," wrote Edmund Starling, Coolidge's Secret Service agent and daily walking companion. "The president was the antithesis of all this and he despised it."[9]

But the president was no reactionary. He did not seek to stand athwart history yelling stop. If he helped mute public enthusiasm for activist government, he didn't significantly roll back the gains of the Progressive Era any more than Eisenhower undid the New Deal or Reagan repealed the Great Society. And if he frowned upon the culture of the 1920s, he smiled contentedly at the rising living standards that made it all possible. Indeed, like his friends Henry Ford, the automaker who clung to ideals of an agrarian past while championing cutting-edge business practices, and Bruce Barton, the adman who reconciled the Christian ideal of salvation with the consumer culture's imperative to spend and enjoy, Calvin Coolidge bridged the zeitgeists of two eras. His modern aspects, though underappreciated, are as significant as his traditional ones.[10]

Coolidge hailed an economy of unprecedented dynamism—what observers were calling the "New Era." As automation spelled the end of artisanal and skilled labor jobs (and as work became less a calling than a form of employment), shorter workweeks, increased leisure time, and rising living standards ushered in a new ethic of consumption. Productive and socially responsible industries, it was hoped—aided by technology and efficient management methods—would deliver material comfort to a growing number of citizens. Americans now placed their increasingly plentiful choices about what to buy for their homes, their families, and themselves at the center of their identity. Spending and buying became a form of freedom under capitalism and a ticket to the good life. F. Scott Fitzgerald would call it "the greatest, gaudiest spree in history." Others called it the Coolidge Prosperity.[11]

Notwithstanding his largely top-down conception of political economy, Coolidge took pride in the middle class's acquisition of new amenities and its apparent attainment of the good life. He welcomed the go-go consumption even as he shared widespread fears about moral decay. Indeed, it was precisely by epitomizing old-fashioned values—by demonstrating that they could survive amid the new consumerism—that Coolidge was able to cheer on the New Era. He offered the public, Lippmann wrote, a "Puritanism de luxe, in which it is possible to praise all the classic virtues while continuing to enjoy all the modern conveniences."[12]

Coolidge accommodated himself to a different aspect of modernity by speaking directly to the public to galvanize popular opinion behind his presidency. "Decisions in the modern state tend to be made by the interaction, not of Congress and the executive, but of public opinion and the executive," Lippmann noted in 1920. "Government tends to operate by the impact of controlled opinion upon administration." Like Theodore Roosevelt and Woodrow Wilson before him, Coolidge governed mainly in this fashion, through what his aide Campbell Bascom Slemp called "direct reliance upon the mass of the people." As his vice president, Charles Dawes, explained, "The popularity of Coolidge . . . is due to the fact that he, not [Congress], best understood the people and they him."[13]

Coolidge's frequent public appeals helped him maintain his popularity. His addresses were less finely reasoned arguments than reassuring homilies, but they disposed people to feel positively about him and the country. Indeed, for a supposedly silent man, many of the highlights of his life centered on speaking. He won praise for the valedictories he delivered to his high school and college classes, and the key piece of campaign literature in his gubernatorial and presidential bids was a collection of his speeches called *Have Faith in Massachusetts*. As president, he pioneered the use of radio to broadcast major addresses, in which his high-pitched New England twang, however unimpressive it might have been in a large hall, pleased living-room listeners with its lack of pretension.

At first blush Coolidge's reticence and the weight he placed on speaking seem contradictory. In fact, they help explain each other. Coolidge succeeded as a communicator precisely because he labored over his speeches, chose his words carefully, and kept his comments simple. "Above all, be brief," he said in his inaugural address to the Massachusetts state senate as president of the body—advice he heeded himself. As president, he would prove a welcome contrast to his bombastic predecessor, Harding, whose typical speech the Democratic politician William McAdoo described as "an army of pompous phrases moving over the landscape in search of an idea." Coolidge also indulged the White House press corps, which was growing in size and influence. He held 520 presidential press conferences, meeting with reporters more regularly than any chief executive before or since.[14]

Presaging the Hollywood stagecraft of Reagan's White House, Coolidge also made use of newsreels, happily posing for cameras filming him performing chores at his Vermont homestead. The leading public relations men of his day—Bruce Barton, a close and trusted friend, and Edward Bernays, an occasional adviser—came to the White House bearing advice and schemes. Coolidge understood public relations not tactically but strategically, as a means for resting his presidency on broad popular support—making him, in this sense, a truly modern president.

. . .

Notwithstanding Coolidge's frequent public comments, and the care that went into forging his "Silent Cal" image, his taciturnity was no myth: Coolidge was fiercely unrevealing about his personal thoughts and feelings. His speeches and press conferences, however copious, fail to shed much light on the inner man. According to one scholar's analysis of twenty-two Coolidge speeches, the president used the word *I* only once in some 52,094 words. "What Coolidge thinks of himself I daresay will never be known," wrote Mencken. "His self-revelations have been so few and so wary that it is even difficult to guess. No august man of his station ever talked about himself less." Even in private conversations, Coolidge kept his guard up. In a rare moment of self-disclosure, he once said that his inveterate shyness predated even the deaths of his mother and his sister, both of whom passed away when he was a boy.[15]

This interiority, which gave rise to talk of the "Coolidge enigma," has long frustrated biographers. "In common with everyone else at Washington, I have been eager to pluck out the heart of Mr. Coolidge's mystery, to discover what sort of a man he is, to establish a basis for appraisal," wrote Edward Lowry in the *New Republic* magazine in 1921, shortly after Coolidge became vice president. "All in vain, for he has revealed nothing, disclosed nothing." In the record handed down to later generations, he remains isolated, remote. Even the best biographies contain few examples of interactions with friends and aides, sustained glimpses of his social life, or evidence of his private thoughts. Though his wife, Grace, appears in some accounts, his two sons are nearly invisible. In Coolidge's own autobiography, he mentions them four times apiece.[16]

Coolidge's silence itself has to be appreciated as a telltale expression of his restrained character. "His outward reticence and aloofness," wrote Edmund Starling, perceptively, "were part of a protective shell." This reserve was evident to everyone who met him. Five feet nine inches tall, slender, with wispy sandy hair and a pallid complexion, Coolidge was moderately handsome but not imposing. He had fine, bony features, a strong cleft chin, pale blue eyes, and a thin downturned line of a mouth that gave him an undeniable air of sternness. "He was splendidly null," wrote a friend from his lawyering days in Northampton, Massachusetts, before he rose to be governor, "apparently deficient in red corpuscles, with a peaked, wire-drawn expression." Arizona congressman Lewis Douglas described him as looking "much like a wooden Indian except more tired-looking." The plain demeanor and upright bearing seemed to reflect his deep-rooted rectitude and modesty.[17]

Described as "an eloquent listener," one who "could be silent in five languages," Coolidge never overcame his shyness. His fondness for cigars, a signature trait noted by many White House visitors, suggested a man who liked having his mouth stuffed so he didn't have to speak; the journalist Bruce Bliven recalled an interview in which the president, in response to each question, would "tilt his head back, holding his long thin Yankee stogie at the angle of an anti-aircraft gun, and think." "Life was largely a mental experience" for him, Starling wrote. Stories and wry comments about Coolidge's taciturnity are legendary. One of the best known concerns the writer Dorothy Parker's reaction to his death, in 1933. Informed of Coolidge's passing, the Algonquin Table wit didn't miss a beat: "How could they tell?" she asked.[18]

Coolidge's muteness is especially striking because he chose an extrovert's profession. But even in the world of politics he found justifications, both philosophical and tactical, for his reticence. "The words of the president have an enormous weight and ought not to be used indiscriminately," he wrote in his autobiography, which is short and unrevealing. In dealing with callers, Coolidge told his successor, Herbert Hoover, silence truly is golden: "If you keep dead still, they will run down in three or four minutes. If you even cough or smile they will start up all over again." To the financier Bernard Baruch, he gave similar counsel. "Well, Baruch, many times I say only 'yes' or 'no' to people. Even this is too much. It winds them up for twenty minutes or more." The silence redounded to his benefit. Coolidge's reserve impressed the public as the hallmark of a safe, steady leader. It allowed different citizens to project onto him their own commonsense wisdom.[19]

Coolidge could be chatty on occasion. Though hardly a natural conversationalist, he charmed guests. One visitor, Cordell Hull, the chairman of the Democratic National Committee (and later Franklin Delano Roosevelt's secretary of state), reported that in a meeting he had with Coolidge, the president "talked freely and easily . . . and was as affable as I could have wished." To conclude, moreover, that because Coolidge was stiff he was also humorless is a mistake.

Indeed, the instances of Coolidge's comic instinct sometimes crowd out serious discussions of his policies. One of his wife's favorite tales was that of the hostess who, aware of the president's reputation for pithiness, beseeched him at an event, "I made a bet today that I could get more than two words out of you." Coolidge's reply: "You lose." As Will Rogers noted, "Mr. Coolidge had a more subtle humor than almost any public man I ever met."[20] In public and private, Coolidge honed an underappreciated wit whose soul truly was its brevity.*

Coolidge's restraint surfaced in other ways, too. Intellectually, he was smart but never daring; Columbia University president Nicholas Murray Butler, who admired Coolidge, charged that he was "wholly lacking in imagination," a harsh but not inaccurate assessment. Socially, he was withdrawn; serving as vice president when the office's main duty was to lead the Senate, "he made no friends among the Senators," wrote Oswald Garrison Villard in the *Nation*, "and ate his lunch from a tin box in a corner of a committee room." Even in lighter moments, Coolidge remained poker-faced. "He never smiled when he was telling a joke or making a witty remark," noted Starling.[21]

Coolidge matched this economy of speech with an economy of money—not just in the policies he promulgated but in his personal habits. He pared back opulent White House dinner menus and made cheese sandwiches for his bodyguard when they went on afternoon walks—grousing, perhaps in jest, that "I have to furnish the cheese." Never an ideologue—he was too unreflective to fall prey to the seductions of an all-encompassing theory—Coolidge built his belief system on the Victorian virtues he had imbibed in his youth. Of course, teaching a boy that waste is a moral wrong, as

---

*The Coolidge wit has given rise to a term in biology, "the Coolidge Effect." According to a story—probably apocryphal—Coolidge and his wife were touring a farm when Mrs. Coolidge was told that a rooster mated several times a day. "Be sure to tell that to the president!" she said. Coolidge then asked whether the rooster mated with the same hen every time, and was told no, it was a different hen each time. "Tell that," he said, "to Mrs. Coolidge." The Coolidge Effect describes the tendency of male animals to be aroused by new females.

Coolidge's father did, need not turn him into a fiscal conservative; but in Coolidge's case, private and public parsimony shared common roots in the New England soil.[22]

They were connected, too, to Coolidge's hands-off, solitary style of governing. "Coolidge had no cabinet of any kind," said White House usher Irwin "Ike" Hoover, "he went [at] it alone in all things." He convened no brainstorming groups or bull sessions in his White House to float ideas, run through hypotheticals, or hear out policy options. Instead, he simply delegated decisions to trusted subordinates. His first "rule of action," he wrote, was "never do . . . anything that someone else can do for you." He handed Treasury Secretary Andrew Mellon the reins of economic policy; Secretaries of State Charles Evans Hughes and Frank Kellogg drove foreign policy; and Herbert Hoover at Commerce grabbed control of as many new projects as he could. Coolidge rarely overrode or questioned their decisions.[23]

Notwithstanding this relative isolation, Coolidge had aides to whom he turned. He commanded deep loyalty from a team of old hands from Massachusetts, such as the businessmen Frank Stearns and William Butler, and from fellow Amherst graduates like the financier Dwight Morrow and the attorney Harlan Fiske Stone. Chief Justice William Howard Taft, the former president, also gave counsel, as did senior staffers such as Bascom Slemp, the White House secretary (the equivalent in those days of chief of staff); Everett Sanders, Slemp's successor; and Edward "Ted" Clark, Coolidge's personal secretary. These colleagues did not form a bustling, dynamic White House. They tended, rather, to reinforce the president's traditional ideas and cautious leadership style. In the main (though not to a man) members of a well-to-do WASP elite, they were conservative but not reactionary, rather like Coolidge himself.

· · ·

In Coolidge's personality lay the fundaments of how he would govern as president. Sparing in words, money, and effort, he was also, in the end, sparing in vision, without great aspirations for his presidency. Compared to the activist Theodore Roosevelt, the visionary

Woodrow Wilson, or even the flamboyant Warren Harding, Coolidge was unambitious—lacking an ennobling idea of how to improve the country or even much of a positive program. In this regard, to be sure, he was hardly out of step with his times; only after the New Deal would Americans demand sweeping programs from their leaders. Hewing to earlier norms, Coolidge thought that the federal government shouldn't do anything that state or local government—or, better yet, the private sphere—could handle. "If the federal government were to go out of existence," he once said, "the common run of people would not detect the difference." He maintained that "the states are the sheet anchors of our institutions."[24]

If this judgment was defensible in the nineteenth century, by the 1920s it was becoming obsolete. The first decades of the new century had transformed the role of the federal government and the presidency. Progressive Era reforms had made Washington responsible for a host of new realms of commerce and industry. America's rise to global stature carried unavoidable commitments. Roosevelt and Wilson had arrogated power to the White House; even under Harding the office had grown, with the landmark 1921 Budget Act tasking the president with setting a policy agenda and accounting for its costs. The president was now an indispensable actor in keeping the country affluent, strong, and just. Whatever his ideology, that duty could not be abdicated. Coolidge, who embraced the flowering of modernity in other respects, didn't understand this new reality.

The limited conception of government's role had the effect of serving business above all. In important ways Coolidge's economic philosophy did resemble the old laissez-faire doctrine: he favored regulating business lightly, cutting taxes, containing federal expenditures, and using budget surpluses to reduce the debt. In other respects, however—such as his support for high tariffs on imports—Coolidge's policies might be more accurately called Hamiltonian, with government purposefully promoting the interests of private manufacturers and finance. Indeed, Coolidge described Hamilton's economic creed as central to the Republican Party of the 1920s:

"The party now in power . . . is representative of those policies which were adopted under the lead of Alexander Hamilton," he said. "This doctrine our party . . . still applies to the business regulations of this republic, not that business may be hampered but that it may be free, not that it may be restricted but that it may expand." Whereas Coolidge regarded the claims of minority groups— immigrants or workers, veterans or African-Americans—as distinct from, and secondary to, the well-being of the majority, he saw the needs of business (for whom, ironically, the term "special interests" had originally been coined) as largely congruent to that of the public as a whole. "I have been greatly pleased to observe," Coolidge noted, "that the attitude of the Chamber of Commerce very accurately reflects that of public opinion generally." After all, unleashing corporate productivity would shower bounty on all of society. And in the short term, events appeared to validate his policies, as the flurry of consumption in the 1920s—and, later in the decade, a spiral of stock-market speculation—goosed the economy and gave the decade its heady rush.[25]

Coolidge's narrow conception of his role as president also led him to stay largely on the sidelines of the decade's culture wars. Although not a temperance crusader, he accepted Prohibition without fuss and let it be known that (unlike Harding) he obeyed the law. He shared none of the bigotry of the revived Ku Klux Klan, yet he never managed to summon a rousing denunciation of that noxious fraternity. He laudably commuted the sentences of members of the Industrial Workers of the World still languishing in jails for their World War I dissent, but he declined to intervene on behalf of Nicola Sacco and Bartolomeo Vanzetti, the anarchist immigrants sentenced to death for murder in Massachusetts, deeming their case a state affair. When contentious social issues did become federal matters, Coolidge typically adopted a moderate conservative stance. He endorsed antilynching laws but didn't fight hard for them, and, in one of his most consequential acts as president, he signed a 1924 law that severely limited immigration, especially from ethnic groups deemed undesirable.[26]

Diffidence and moderation similarly colored Coolidge's foreign policy. Neither a Wilsonian internationalist nor a defiant isolationist, he supported efforts to work with Europe and Japan to build a more peaceful future, though in most cases he pressed his cause too lightly, or adopted goals too ephemeral, to yield lasting gains. He avoided the League of Nations debate, backed down in his efforts to get the United States to join the World Court, and failed to build on Harding's arms limitations treaties. The major agreements he did strike—the 1924 Dawes Plan addressing European debt and the 1928 Kellogg-Briand Pact promising to "outlaw war"—were hailed in their day but turned out to be toothless once Europe's crises worsened. Just as the Depression would occasion recriminations about Coolidge's economic agenda, so the resumption of hostilities abroad in the 1930s would discredit international policies that had once seemed the essence of wisdom.

Coolidge's record, in sum, was neither substantial nor enduring. Too many problems, left unaddressed, mounted; too many causes languished unpursued. His constricted vision of his office crippled him.

And yet, as Coolidge knew, a president's achievement does not lie merely in the laws and policies he implements. What also counts is how a president gauges, guides, and gives expression to the mood of the people he leads. Here is where Coolidge's success lies. Most Americans viewed him as levelheaded if not extraordinary, virtuous if not visionary—a man whose presence in the White House offered sustenance and calm. Embodying the cherished ideals of a fading order while giving silent benediction to the ethos of a new age, Coolidge was a transitional president at a transitional time. In his anxious acceptance of the era's ballyhoo and roar, in the quiet pleasure he took in beholding the fruits of American industry, in the solitary sadness he felt in trying to treasure a lost world—in all these ways he reflected and defined the 1920s. To understand that critical decade, then, it is necessary to reckon with Calvin Coolidge, the thirtieth president of the United States.

1

Out of Plymouth Notch

Calvin Coolidge remembered the rustic world of his boyhood, not altogether romantically, as a lost arcadia. He was born on the Fourth of July, in 1872, seven years after the end of the Civil War. He grew up, like his parents, in Plymouth Notch, Vermont, a village of farmhouses nestled in the Green Mountains. It had 1,300 residents, almost all of Yankee descent.

Typical of rural America, living conditions in Plymouth Notch were rough and rugged. Frigid winters dragged on for months. No gas lamps, running water, or coal furnaces relieved the hardship. Taxing labor—building fences, tending the animals, tapping trees to make syrup—fell even upon young boys like Calvin.

Coolidge, however, remembered not the hardship but an idyllic life of county fairs, bobsledding on snowy slopes, romps over the green hills, a well-taught pride in executing his chores, and blissful nights under starry skies. "Vermont is my birthright," he later reminisced. "Here one gets close to nature, in the mountains, in the brooks, the waters of which hurry to the sea."[1]

The Coolidge family shared the attitudes common to the region: the Puritan piety, the esteem for hard work and thrift, and what Coolidge recalled as the refusal to show disdain toward others "except toward those who assumed superior airs." The Yankee political culture included both conservative and progressive strains. The first state to abolish slavery, Vermont prided itself on its religiously rooted egalitarianism, though its lack of racial and ethnic diversity made such tolerance a mostly abstract affair. Indeed, Vermonters looked warily upon the unruly, ethnically diverse Democratic Party, with its immigrants, wage earners, and urbanites. For them, the Party of Lincoln embodied their values of civic duty and robust individualism. Though hardly shrill in his partisanship, Coolidge never questioned which party merited his loyalty. Even when he was a teenager, he recalled, party affinities among Vermonters were sufficiently monolithic that Republican Benjamin Harrison's presidential victory in 1888 over the incumbent Democrat Grover Cleveland gave rise to unalloyed festivity at his high school. "Two nights were spent parading the streets with drums and trumpets," Coolidge wrote, "celebrating the victory." Vermont would retain its Republican allegiance even through the New Deal—favoring the GOP presidential candidate in every election until Lyndon B. Johnson won the state for the Democrats as part of his 1964 landslide.[2]

Yankee Republicanism seemed to run in the Coolidge blood. Before Calvin's birth, the town of Plymouth and the outlying "Notch" had served as home to four generations of Coolidges; the family traced its ancestry to the Puritans who first came to Massachusetts in the early seventeenth century. Plymouth was where Calvin's parents, John Calvin Coolidge and Victoria Moor, first met and where in 1868 they were married. When their first child, the future president, arrived four years later, the Coolidges gave him John's full name but chose to refer to him as Calvin. (Later, in an act of mildest rebellion, Coolidge would drop the "John" altogether.) In 1875, Victoria gave birth to a sister for Calvin named Abigail.

John Coolidge was a jack-of-all-trades. Though tending a farm was a full-time job, he rarely went without other work. He ran the town's general store when Calvin was born but soon sold it and bought the farmhouse across the way. Moved by the New England esteem for public service, John went on to hold, as one admirer remarked, every local or state office "except the undertaker": he served as selectman, school commissioner, tax collector, constable, deputy sheriff, and eventually state representative and state senator.[3]

Calvin revered his father and imbibed his sense of duty and mission. "My father had qualities that were greater than any I possess," Calvin later insisted. "He was a man of untiring industry and great tenacity of purpose." As a boy Calvin accompanied John to the courthouse and to town meetings. These experiences instilled what he called "a good working knowledge of the practical side of government" and a view of politics as noble.[4]

Coolidge was close to his mother as well. Fair-haired and sentimental like her son, she loved to plant flowers, "gaze at the purple sunsets, and watch the evening stars," he recalled. But as long as he could remember, she suffered from tuberculosis, and she died in 1885, at the age of thirty-nine, after having been injured by a runaway horse. Following her death, Coolidge wrote, "life was never to seem the same again." Although he rarely disclosed his emotions, he spoke effusively about her throughout his life. To Edmund Starling, the president's bodyguard and friend, Coolidge seemed able to recall "every day he had spent with her." "I wish I could really speak to her," the president told Starling. "I wish that often." Coolidge kept his mother's photograph on his desk and carried with him a locket that held a lock of her hair.[5]

Five years after the loss of his mother, Coolidge's sister, Abbie, also died, probably from appendicitis, at the age of fourteen. She had recently joined Calvin as a student at the Black River Academy in nearby Ludlow, where she was his favorite companion. Her sudden loss—she died within a week of taking ill—was nearly as shattering as that of his mother. Beyond the obvious grief, the precise effect of these traumas on Calvin is hard to determine. They didn't create his inclination to diffidence or his fear of the unplanned, which had been in evidence from a young age. But they must have reinforced those traits. For the rest of his life, Calvin would remain deliberate in his decisions, conservative in his temperament and ideology, and restrained in his personal style.

Coolidge's eventual choice of a life in politics represented a triumph of his ambition and his admiration for his father over the shyness he felt so acutely as a boy. "It's a hard thing for me to play this game," he told Frank Stearns, the Massachusetts department store mogul he befriended at mid-career. "In politics, one must meet people, and that's not easy for me. . . . When I was a little fellow, as long ago as I can remember, I would go into a panic if I heard strange voices in the house. I felt I just couldn't meet the people and shake hands with them. Most of the visitors would sit with Mother and Father in the kitchen and the hardest thing in the world was to have to go through the kitchen door and give them a greeting. . . . I'm all right with old friends, but every time I meet a stranger, I've got to go through the old kitchen door, back home, and it's not easy."[6]

• • •

In his autobiography, Coolidge mentions no childhood friends. Biographers cite no significant relationships outside his family until he got to college. His experience at Black River, where he enrolled in February 1886, at age thirteen, was often solitary. A wallflower at school social events, he wrote to his father about his homesickness, and on weekends he frequently returned to Plymouth Notch to see his father or visited an aunt and uncle in a nearby town.

Gradually, though, Coolidge's social skills improved. He began to display his winning mischievousness. In his autobiography, he looked back on his adolescent pranks with appropriately measured pride. "One morning as the janitor was starting the furnace he heard a loud bray from one of the classrooms," Coolidge recalled, where the worker discovered "a domestic animal noted for his long ears and discordant voice. In some way during the night he had been stabled on the second floor." In one of the memoir's rare flashes of his dry wit, Coolidge added, "About as far as I deem it prudent to discuss my own connection with these escapades is to record that I was never convicted of any of them and so must be presumed innocent."[7]

Besides finding his stride socially at Black River, Coolidge also improved academically. Following a college preparatory curriculum, he studied Greek and Latin, as well as history and politics, his favorite subjects. He distinguished himself enough to be asked to deliver a graduation address. His talk, titled "Oratory in History," with its high praise for Cicero and Demosthenes, Patrick Henry and Daniel Webster, suggested that for all Coolidge's reticence, he found public speaking compelling. The address touted the power of rhetoric to shape history. "It was not the fleets of Attica, though mighty, nor the valor of her troops, though unconquerable, that diverted her destinies," Coolidge pronounced, "but the words and gestures of men who had the genius and skill to move, to concentrate, and to direct the energies and passions of a whole people." If grandiloquent to modern ears, Coolidge's performance impressed the crowd. A local newspaper reporter called it "masterly in its conception and arrangement." For the rest of his life, in both state and national politics, Silent Cal would fight past his shyness to surprise doubters and win acclaim for his speeches. Although no one ever mistook him for a natural talent, and he never mastered the stirring, crowd-pleasing style of history's great orators, he managed early on to find his voice: restrained, thoughtful, intelligent. Behind the rostrum, his native moderation came through, and audiences seemed to like his performances all the more because they expressed the measured sentiments of someone not given to gratuitous lecturing.[8]

With his strong academic record and his keen ambitions, Coolidge was a natural choice to attend college. Amherst College, not far across the border in western Massachusetts, was a natural choice for Black River graduates. When Coolidge took the entrance exam, however, he was ill and failed to complete it, and he was denied admission. Undeterred, he undertook another term of preparatory study, at the nearby St. Johnsbury Academy, whose well-connected principal then helped arrange the young man's admission to Amherst. He matriculated in 1891, at the age of nineteen.[9]

At college, Coolidge followed a trajectory similar to his path in high school, starting off socially isolated but finding a place for himself over his four years. A respectable student, he continued to study history, politics, and oratory, taking classes in declamation, rhetoric, public speaking, and debate. Coolidge also fell under the influence of a philosophy professor with a cult following on campus. Charles

Garman was no scholar but an immensely popular tutor who preached a homegrown brand of Christian humanism that emphasized spirituality, self-reliance, and industry. During Coolidge's presidency, the journalist Frederick Lewis Allen would mock these "old American copybook maxims . . . brought down from some Vermont attic where *McGuffey's Reader* gathered dust," but students at Amherst lapped up the wisdom that Garman imparted through his Socratic classroom style. "No doubt there are those who think they can demonstrate that this teaching was not correct," Coolidge later conceded in recalling the devotion to Garman's home-published pamphlets, which substituted for books on the syllabus. "With them I have no argument. I know that in experience it has worked." Coolidge's preference for experience over ideas was a deeply rooted trait.[10]

As in high school, Coolidge's peers found him withdrawn and insecure. "He lacked small talk, and he was never known, I suspect, to slap a man on the back," recalled a classmate. "He rarely laughed. He was anything but a mixer." Over time, however, Coolidge made some good friends, including Dwight Morrow and Harlan Fiske Stone, both of whom he would later appoint to high government posts. His classmates came to appreciate his deadpan wit and talent for speech making, which he developed through conscientious application in and out of class. In his junior year he shared the prize for the best orator in the class, and at the end of his senior year he not only won Latin academic honors, graduating cum laude, but was chosen by his peers to deliver the Grove Oration, a humorous send-up of the senior class, at commencement.[11]

At his father's urging, Coolidge pursued a career in law. Shortly after graduation, he went for a walk with Morrow to discuss life after college. Morrow said he planned to go to law school at Pittsburgh. But Coolidge preferred to stay closer to home; he remained very much attached to his father (who had remarried in 1891, to a local woman, Carrie Brown) and to the area. When Morrow asked him where he planned to study, Coolidge replied, "Northampton is the nearest courthouse." In 1895, attending law school wasn't necessary to practice at the bar; aspiring lawyers still often "read" law under the tutelage of practicing attorneys, and Coolidge preferred practical training to academic study. Northampton became his new home.[12]

. . .

Coolidge apprenticed himself to two Amherst graduates, John Hammond and Henry Field, who ran a small firm and had been charmed by the young man's wit. They specialized in humdrum work such as real estate, wills, and small-time litigation—work for which Coolidge, with his sober diligence, proved abundantly suited. After two years at the firm, Coolidge passed the bar in 1897, just before his twenty-fifth birthday.

On the surface, Coolidge didn't seem destined for great things. But beneath his quiet exterior, ambitions surged. Hammond and Field were active in local politics, and within a year Coolidge, benefiting from their connections, set his sights on office. In 1898 he was elected to the Northampton city council—as a Republican, naturally. For the next thirty years he would remain, almost uninterrupted, a holder of public office.

Coolidge's rise in local, state, and national politics was as methodical as it was swift. He rarely held a position for more than a couple of years before climbing to the next rung. From 1898 to 1928, he lost only one race, in 1905—for the Northampton school board. Undeterred, he ran the next year for the state legislature and won. Northampton elected him mayor in 1909; he lowered municipal taxes and shrank the city debt while raising teachers' salaries. In 1911 he won election to the state senate and within two years became president of the body—and a power in state politics.

Coolidge's ascent baffled those observers who found it hard to see past the vapors of ordinariness he exuded. During his presidency, critics would ascribe his success to luck, to being at the right place at the right time. But luck is often the residue of design, and Coolidge "meant to be ready to take advantage of opportunities," as he put it. Nor did his critics always appreciate that anti-politics can be a smart form of politics—that a lack of panache can confer the air of competence and integrity that voters seek. In his early races, Coolidge had to force himself to introduce himself to strangers; as president he would endure state dinners and depart at the first possible moment. But throughout it all Coolidge never seemed to be someone he wasn't.[13]

As incongruous as Coolidge's forced glad-handing was his marriage in 1905 to Grace Goodhue, invariably described as vivacious and judged by Edmund Starling "the personification of charm." A Phi Beta Kappa graduate of the University of Vermont and a teacher at the Clarke Institute for the Deaf in Northampton, Grace had an olive complexion, lush black hair, and all the social ease her husband lacked. Coolidge's courtship of her initiated his first serious romantic relationship, and the two were wed within two years of meeting.[14]

With her warmth and friendliness, Grace often brought out Calvin's lighter side. Despite her New England roots, she lacked his flintiness; on the contrary, her gaiety won over many who found her husband unbearably dour. Later she would delight Washington society with her style and poise. Their marriage would provide an important anchor to Coolidge—all the more solid because Grace wasn't deeply involved in his career. Like his religious faith, she gave him a reservoir of strength and security cordoned off from political affairs.

The young couple moved into half of a two-family house in Northampton. They stayed there, living in Coolidge's trademark frugal manner, until he became vice president, and they would return there after his presidency. "The process of my domestication," Grace recalled, "was undertaken almost immediately," as she learned to darn socks and master other household chores. Soon, two sons were born: John on September 7, 1906, and Calvin Jr. on April 13, 1908. From the beginning, Coolidge seemed to favor the younger boy, whose delicate physique, blue eyes, and reddish hair gave him a distinct resemblance to his father. Coolidge related to both boys by joking and teasing, but they reacted to his japes

differently. While Calvin Jr. learned to mimic his father's style
and tease back, the thin-skinned John felt wounded by his father's
ribbing.[15]

Coolidge's severe style of parenting, not uncommon for the
age, stemmed from his old-fashioned conception of fatherhood. He
sought above all to instill his code of discipline, diligence, and responsibility. Loving but stern, he laid down strict rules about how the
boys should dress, study, and even pray. On at least a few occasions
he hit them. Both boys took their father's efforts to heart. John,
who lived to be ninety-three, remembered late in life that his father
was "very, very strict." Calvin Jr., who came to share his father's
crisp wit, agreed. In the summer of 1923, when he was working a
job in a tobacco field, another boy discovered Calvin's identity and
remarked: "If my father was president, I would not work in a
tobacco field." To which the boy replied, "If my father were your
father, you would."[16]

Coolidge's parsimony in these years gave rise to much lore. At
their Northampton home, the Coolidges didn't have their own
telephone service but shared a party line. Coolidge saw no reason to
buy a car, even though they were now being produced cheaply and
abundantly. "I had to plan very carefully for a time to live within my
income," he explained. "I know very well what it means to awake in
the night and realize that the rent is coming due, wondering where
the money is coming from."[17]

The same even-keeled determination guided Coolidge's rise.
Besides his charming charmlessness, Coolidge possessed several
underappreciated traits. He refrained from denouncing opponents,
preferring to stress the principles, however banal, underlying his
own positions. He alienated few voters and strengthened his hand
in building coalitions and appealing to different constituencies.
When Theodore Roosevelt broke with the Republican Party to run
for president in 1912 as the candidate of his own Progressive, or
"Bull Moose," Party, he exacerbated a rift in the GOP between its
liberal wing and its conservative, pro-business "Old Guard." In Massachusetts, Coolidge helped heal that breach, not because he was a

Rooseveltian at heart but because he was temperamentally a moderate, palatable to both of the party's warring camps. Coolidge's relatively liberal record in the state senate on certain progressive keystones—he supported women's suffrage and the direct election of senators, for example—earned him the confidence, if not the enthusiastic support, of GOP progressives and even some Democrats.

At the same time, Coolidge forged relationships with influential Massachusetts businessmen and power brokers. Most important was Frank Stearns, the owner of an eponymous department store and an Amherst man sixteen years Coolidge's senior, who became a key patron. For the rest of Coolidge's career, Stearns would raise and spend money on the politician's behalf, even paying his personal expenses. Stearns also brought business interests into line behind Coolidge, freeing up the rising politician to court other groups. Meanwhile, Coolidge cemented his bond with U.S. Senator Winthrop Murray Crane—a former governor, a force in state Republican politics, and a rival to its other kingfish, Senator Henry Cabot Lodge. Crane's right-hand man, William Butler, a textile manufacturer and former state representative, became a critical ally as well. Crane and Butler's politicking helped Coolidge ascend to the state senate presidency and establish himself as a player on Beacon Hill. Butler would eventually ride Coolidge's coattails to a seat in the U.S. Senate and the chairmanship of the Republican National Committee.

•   •   •

Coolidge became president of the state senate in 1913, at a high tide of political reform. Woodrow Wilson was shepherding progressive legislation through Congress. The militant Industrial Workers of the World were making gains among wage laborers; the year before they had led a successful textile strike in Lawrence, Massachusetts, that Coolidge, as the head of a legislative committee, had mediated. The suffragists Alice Paul and Lucy Burns organized a new party to secure the vote for all women. Two constitutional amendments—introducing the income tax and the direct election of senators—had just been ratified. Public opinion generally backed these progressive causes, even as the middle and upper classes were growing fearful of more radical changes.

In tune with this sentiment, Coolidge supported many progressive reforms even as he worried that change was happening too fast. In his first speech as senate president he warned of extremists and affirmed his belief in the soundness of the system. Dubbed "Have Faith in Massachusetts," the speech represented another instance of the taciturn politician using the rostrum to his advantage. His address struck a chord, brought him acclaim, and made him a contender for lieutenant governor, a largely honorific position that nonetheless served as a stepping-stone to the governor's chair. Coolidge thought the post worth pursuing, and in 1915 he was elected on a ticket headed by Samuel McCall, a former congressman. Coolidge bided his time through three one-year stints as lieutenant governor until, in 1918, McCall stepped aside. Coolidge was now the front-runner to lead the Commonwealth of Massachusetts.

Like Vermont, Massachusetts in 1918 was heavily Republican, with strong Yankee traditions. Coolidge won endorsements from most of the state's newspapers and by all rights should have been elected in a cakewalk. But Boston and the industrial cities in the eastern part of the state were swelling with immigrants and trending Democratic. What was more, the Democratic nominee, a Framingham shoe merchant named Richard Long, played for the workingmen's vote, assailing Coolidge as a shill for business. With Wilson having led the country into the First World War in April 1917, patriotism was becoming a favorite issue of demagogues, and Long insinuated that Coolidge wasn't fully behind the war effort. Although Coolidge wished to stick to the high road, and did so more or less, he wasn't immune to the pressures of wartime pandering. He engaged in his share of bashing "the German military despotism" and "its conspiracy against mankind," as if to prove his patriotic bona fides. Ultimately, he squeaked out a victory of 214,000 votes to Long's 197,000—the slimmest margin of his career.[18]

The narrowness of Coolidge's win, however, didn't obscure the impressive slope of his ascent. At forty-six, he had reached the pinnacle of state politics. "My progress had been slow and toilsome," he wrote with characteristic modesty, "with little about it that was brilliant, or spectacular, the result of persistent and painstaking work." His responsiveness to the public temper—showing strains of progressivism, of anti-radicalism, and of war hawkishness each when the times demanded—and his blend of caution and unobtrusive ambition had served him well. They would continue to do so in the years ahead.[19]

2

―――――――

On the Brink

In his years in Massachusetts government, Coolidge had conducted his business at the statehouse in Boston while maintaining his small Northampton home across the state, where Grace and their two sons stayed. In Boston, Coolidge rented a room for a dollar and a half a night at the Adams House hotel. After he was elected governor, however, a change in lifestyle was in order. Since Massachusetts provided for no governor's mansion, Coolidge arranged to rent a second room at the Adams House, for another dollar a night.[1]

Every indication suggested that Coolidge would govern as simply as he lived. Besides keeping his modest lodgings, he was known to arrive at events by streetcar (anticipating the unpretentious commuting habits of a later Massachusetts governor, Michael Dukakis). He still stood apart from Boston's Brahmin aristocracy, still lunched with friends and businessmen at the Union Club, still politicked quietly but ably. Even now he struck observers as a lesser figure than Massachusetts's other leading officeholders—Murray Crane, Coolidge's mentor in state politics, and Henry Cabot Lodge, then mobilizing to defeat President Wilson's plans to join the new League of Nations. Unlike these titans, Coolidge shunned high-profile or controversial roles. When Wilson visited Boston on his return from peace talks in France in February 1919, Governor Coolidge welcomed him and struck a middle-of-the-road stance, calling for American entry into the League provided that various amendments to the treaty could be passed. A month later, Coolidge moderated a debate about the League between Lodge and Harvard president A. Lawrence Lowell. "Both men won," Coolidge pronounced at the end.[2]

Moderation was Coolidge's watchword. In state affairs he stressed efficiency, honesty, and harmony. He tried to reduce taxes. He vetoed a bill to raise legislators' salaries by 50 percent and other measures to upgrade the Boston ferry and to widen a South Boston thoroughfare, insisting, with a reasoning that always undergirded his governance, that "the functions of the City Hall ought not to be performed by the State House." Toward the end of his term he vetoed a bill that would have allowed the sale of beer and light wine, considering it to be a violation of Prohibition, established by the Eighteenth Amendment in 1919.[3]

Coolidge leavened his fiscal conservatism with the progressive impulses he had shown as a legislator. He signed into law measures to improve working conditions, regulate landlords, fund new forests, and control outdoor advertising. He endorsed bills crossing his desk that provided bonuses, hiring preferences, and other benefits to returning veterans, though he opposed more sweeping measures to guarantee them jobs. And his most significant feat as governor married progressivism's efficiency to conservatism's taste for small government: he restructured the state government, consolidating in a single year more than one hundred agencies into fewer than twenty.

Coolidge's commitment to his work routinely kept him from his wife and sons. "While our boys were growing up," Grace later recalled, "their father sacrificed much in devoting himself so diligently to his public duties that he was unable to be with them as much as he would have liked." He missed birthdays and other special occasions. But as he taught his sons, hard work was unavoidable for men who wished to make something of themselves.[4]

·   ·   ·

Coolidge's record as governor was creditable but not strong enough to advance his own ambitions. To propel himself to national prominence, he needed something more—a transformative event. That

opportunity arrived late in the summer of 1919 with the Boston
police strike. This was the year of the first Red Scare, a national
panic about Bolshevism and anarchism, prompted by the Russian
Revolution abroad and radical violence at home. Fueling the anxiety
was an outbreak of labor agitation, itself fed by a postwar dynamic
of surging prices and comparatively stagnant wages. During the
year, some four million Americans walked off their jobs as part of
an estimated 2,665 strikes, including an industry-wide strike by
350,000 steel workers. Though a spirit of reform persisted in many
quarters, it was now more than counterbalanced by the new fear of
radical change.

These conditions did not bode well for Boston's policemen.
Poorly paid, saddled with long hours, subject to danger in their
daily work, the officers, mostly Irish-Catholic, resented the city's
English-descent Protestant elite. For months the policemen had
been trying to gain leverage to negotiate for better contracts, but
the police commissioner, a hard-bitten, self-important fifty-nine-
year-old Republican named Edwin Curtis, refused to let them form
a union, contending it could lead to a strike that would jeopardize
public safety. In late August, the policemen's lead negotiators opted
to unionize anyway, affiliating with Samuel Gompers's American
Federation of Labor. Curtis promptly fired the eight police leaders
who had made the deal and had them tried under administrative
procedures. All eight—and soon another eleven—were convicted.

Tensions escalated. Boston mayor Andrew Peters also opposed a
policemen's union, but as a Democrat and a glad-handing politician, he was sensitive to his Irish as well as his Yankee constituents
and more sympathetic to the officers than Curtis was. (Peters had
no direct authority over Curtis, who was appointed by and answer-
able to the governor.) Seeking a compromise, Peters assembled a
committee, led by the prominent banker James Storrow, to find a
solution centering on independent arbitration. To support his plan,
Peters appealed to Governor Coolidge, who was spending the
August doldrums visiting Northampton and Vermont. Peters was
sorely disappointed.

At the time, Coolidge wasn't considered hostile to labor. Although he had planned to seize control of the telephone system when operators threatened to strike earlier in the year, he had also mediated the 1912 Lawrence textile strike to the workers' satisfaction and, earlier in his gubernatorial term, discreetly addressed the grievances of Boston's streetcar men. Nor was Coolidge callous toward the policemen's plight; he had urged improvements in the overcrowded stationhouses. But he declined to be drawn into the police standoff. Through his whole career he would propound a doctrine—part philosophy of government, part management style—that favored delegating responsibility wherever possible and making decisions at upper levels only when necessary. In this case, he deemed the labor negotiations a local affair, essentially siding with Commissioner Curtis, whose view of the matter he privately shared. On Monday, September 8, when Coolidge spoke to the convention of the Massachusetts Federation of Labor in Greenfield, Massachusetts, he didn't even mention the brewing crisis.

He was sticking his head in the sand. At the same meeting, workers resolved to decry "the Hunnish attitude of Police Commissioner Curtis." And on that same Monday, Curtis suspended the nineteen convicted officers, seeding outrage among cops and the Irish working class. Pushed into a corner, the policemen voted 1,134 to 2 the next day to strike. Shortly after five o'clock that evening, 1,117 of Boston's 1,544 cops walked off the beat.[5]

Tuesday's autumn twilight had a nip in the air and a lingering mist after three days of sporadic rain. At first the streets stayed calm. But as news of the strike spread, looters and hooligans gathered in Boston's neighborhoods—South Boston, the North End, and the West End, bordering Beacon Hill—where they drank, threw dice, hollered, stole tires from cars, and harassed pedestrians. After midnight, the tomfoolery escalated into rioting. Young men smashed store windows, raided shops, and wantonly destroyed property. Assured by Curtis that the state militia wasn't needed, Coolidge hadn't mobilized them. Nor did he do so during the night. He slept soundly at Adams House as the mayhem continued in the wee hours.

Despite this negligence, the press (and, it appeared, the public) mostly blamed the police. Even President Wilson fixed fault on the officers, whose abdication of their "sacred and direct" duty, he said, amounted to "a crime against civilization." Bostonians panicked, fearing lawlessness might reign unchecked. Alarmists invoked the specter of Bolshevism. Other workers—firemen, streetcar workers, telephone and telegraph operators—who harbored their own grievances considered joining the strike. On Wednesday night, Mayor Peters called out the Boston units of the state militia, but even with the help of seven hundred Harvard students and other volunteer patrolmen, they couldn't restrain the mobs. Rioting continued. Three men were killed.[6]

On Thursday, after prodding from Crane, Butler, and others, Coolidge belatedly brought out the full State Guard. Order was restored.

Yet the crisis was still to deepen. Piqued, Curtis fired the striking police force, began hiring permanent replacements, and forbade the strikers from reclaiming their old jobs. Coolidge supported these reprisals. On September 12, Gompers telegrammed Coolidge and Peters in a bid to get the policemen their jobs back and resolve the strike. But the governor stood fast. "There is no right to strike against the public safety by anybody, anywhere, any time," he replied to the union president, in a message he cannily released to the press. The pithy pronouncement was classic Coolidge, neatly articulating what struck many as commonsense wisdom with a tautness that made it ripe for repetition in newspapers, newsreels, and conversation. Yet if Coolidge's position had the virtues of clarity and consistency, it didn't justify the punitive measures that he and Curtis had meted out. Even the liberal *New Republic* editorialized that "the police did not deserve to win," but the magazine spoke for progressive opinion in judging the wholesale firings to be "harsh, inexpedient, and wrong-headed."[7]

Nonetheless, Coolidge's rebuke to Gompers, quoted often in the subsequent months, tapped a nationwide vein of antagonism to trade unions. It also underscored the support for his ideal of political harmony, his view that there existed overarching public interests that trumped the sectarian demands of particular groups. The governor reaffirmed his views in a public statement on September 24, adding that to trust the public safety to "men who have attempted to destroy it" would be irresponsible. This stand made Coolidge, almost unwittingly, a national hero. His string-bean figure and dour demeanor appeared in newspapers, accompanied by gushing editorials. Seventy thousand letters and telegrams arrived in Boston bearing tributes.[8]

Though interpreted as decisive, Coolidge's performance actually displayed his trademark passivity. Initially he waited to act, not wanting to usurp local power; then he deferred to Curtis's judgment; then he acted only under pressure. Although his line on the illegality of the strike was consistent, it wasn't until his ringing statements afterward that he was perceived as the leader. Some observers expected that his performance during the ordeal—to say nothing of his tardiness in summoning the militia—would hurt him in his quest for reelection. Coolidge himself feared the fallout might end his political career.

As it turned out, his law-and-order line helped him greatly. "Remember September the 9th," newspaper advertisements implored. Frank Stearns, having contracted with Houghton Mifflin to publish a book of Coolidge's speeches, added to the collection the governor's remarks about the strike; taking its title from Coolidge's 1914 speech "Have Faith in Massachusetts," the volume proved to be one of the more successful campaign books in history. Riding high, Coolidge dispatched Democrat Richard Long that November in a rematch of the 1918 gubernatorial contest, winning by more than 100,000 votes.[9]

In the police strike Coolidge had cast his lot squarely with the middle classes over the working classes, but his behavior cannot be reduced to that of an enemy of labor. What his actions did show were several hallmarks of his governing style. Coolidge preferred restraint to action, and he trusted his appointees, in this case Curtis, rather than overruling them. And although Coolidge harbored progressive tendencies, he was at bottom a New England conservative; he favored modest reforms so long as they neither moved too fast nor disrupted the established order. The police strike offended him not because he had contempt for workingmen but because his belief in civic harmony overrode any urgency he might feel about redressing social inequalities. His philosophy explained how he could, without contradiction, mediate strikes or crush them, depending on the circumstances.

Remarks that Coolidge made toward the end of his term as governor reflected not just pride in his accomplishments but also his idea that a single national good existed, and that politicians should seek to promote that common interest, rather than broker among warring factional interests. "We are reaching and maintaining the position . . . where the property class and the employed class are not separate, but identical," he said in a speech. "There is a relationship of interdependence which makes their interests the same in the long run. . . . This is the ideal economic condition." This view, quite prevalent at the time, was not a reactionary position but a mainstream conservative one—and not too far even from Progressive orthodoxy. Progressives such as Theodore Roosevelt and Woodrow Wilson tended to believe that the proper goal of politics was to satisfy a "general interest," and not the special interests of any particular groups. The Progressives considered business concerns to be among these special interests, but they sometimes put constituencies such as farmers or veterans in that category too. Significantly, Coolidge, who believed that corporate productivity would trickle down to all, did not typically contrast the needs of business with those of the public. Yet he shared the Progressives' conception of a "general" good. Indeed, this notion was central to Coolidge's thought, and it informed his governance in Massachusetts, as it would in Washington.[10]

• • •

The Coolidge persona that emerged from the Boston police strike was that of a level-headed man with firm, commonsense convictions, devoted to the general good. Those qualities, and the attention he received during the episode, put him in the running for president of the United States as the 1920 election neared.

From the start of his gubernatorial tenure, Coolidge's backers—particularly Stearns and Morrow, who in 1914 had become a partner at the J. P. Morgan Bank, the largest in the United States—were strategizing. "I do not know of anything better that can be done to help human beings and to help business than to make Calvin Coolidge the one great leader in the country," Stearns wrote Morrow in January 1919. After his easy reelection, Coolidge too began to think he had a shot. Stearns and Morrow tried to position him for the Republican Party nomination, to be awarded at the national convention in June 1920.[11]

One invaluable asset was the pioneering advertising man Bruce Barton. Just thirty-three at the time, the son of a Congregationalist minister and an Amherst graduate, Barton had shuttled between magazine journalism and advertising in his early years before forming the firm of Barton, Durstine & Osborn in 1919. (George Batten would join them as a partner in 1928, giving the firm the initials under which it would become famous, BBD&O.) A celebrant of business and an apostle of the emerging consumer culture, Barton went on to enjoy a rich and varied career. In 1925 he published *The Man Nobody Knows*, the best-selling book in America for two years running, which reinvented Jesus Christ as a charismatic entrepreneur. Later, he would win election to Congress from Manhattan's Upper East Side "Silk Stocking District," earning in that role a place in Franklin Roosevelt's rogues' gallery of obstructionists, "Martin, Barton and Fish."

Barton began to serve Coolidge as an informal consultant, at a time before full-time political publicist was a known job description. He was introduced to the Massachusetts governor in 1919 by Morrow, a friend of both men, who arranged a meeting in Boston.

Like Coolidge, Barton bridged two eras, fusing a commitment to rural values and an inclination to celebrate the bounty of the New Era. Joining Coolidge's unofficial team, Barton wrote a glowing profile of the governor in the magazine *Collier's*, the first such article in a national publication. "Less than five percent of the people of America today are doing 95 percent of the talking," Barton noted, with a nod to Coolidge's silence. "The radicals and reactionaries fill the newspapers, but the great majority of Americans are neither radicals nor reactionaries. They are middle-of-the-road folks who own their own homes and work hard. . . . Coolidge belongs with that crowd." Over the next decade, the publicist would pen many more of these encomiums for magazines whose editors were either inexcusably blind to Barton's service to Coolidge or shamefully derelict in ignoring it. Barton thus helped forge the image of "Silent Cal," portraying Coolidge's stony New England reserve as a hallmark of his flinty integrity.[12]

Barton's portraits were strategic, designed to stress Coolidge's best qualities. Some critics, after all, viewed Coolidge's diffidence as a bloodless reserve. "Wild Indians could not have tortured a groan or a grin from him," the *Boston Globe* said, reflecting the ethnic insensitivities of the day. But Barton could transform these defects into the virtues of earthiness and sincerity. In one article, he told of Coolidge sitting on a porch when a man in a wagon passed, calling out hello to "Cal." Coolidge replied with his own "Howdy, Newt," and then explained matter-of-factly to Barton: "Cousin of mine. Haven't seen him for twenty years." Evocative photographs illustrated Barton's paeans, including, in Barton's first piece, a shot of Coolidge behind a two-horse hitch at the Vermont family farm.[13]

Coolidge accommodated himself to the publicity blitz. Some historians have viewed Coolidge as guileless at public relations. But he recognized, even as many of his contemporaries did not, that such efforts were part and parcel of modern politics. "In public life it is sometimes necessary," he wrote in his autobiography, "in order to appear really natural, to be actually artificial." Long before the term "photo op" was coined, stories surfaced of the governor's pliability for the cameras. "Let's spruce up a bit," he suggested to Frank Stearns before they posed for the lenses. "And let's talk. It looks more natural and makes a better picture."[14]

Barton, meanwhile, was indefatigable. Eyeing the upcoming 1920 convention, he placed pro-Coolidge ads in cities that hosted state caucuses to choose their delegates. He churned out articles targeting women, pamphlets aimed at teachers, and brochures meant for delegates, to whom Stearns was sending, at his own expense, copies of *Have Faith in Massachusetts*—all with Coolidge's assent. Barton arranged for Coolidge supporters around the country to write to *Literary Digest* urging the magazine to include the governor in its series of profiles of presidential aspirants. It did.

Held in Chicago from June 8 to 12, the 1920 Republican National Convention was wide open, in the style of the rowdy party conclaves of the nineteenth century. Despite his new fame, Coolidge wasn't among the top contenders. He lacked a strong, identifiable base that could work for him as a bloc, and because of the long odds of his nomination and his diffident nature, he declined to lobby hard for the nod. Instead he assumed the posture of a noncandidate, leaving open the chance of being drafted in case of a convention deadlock—a scenario that Barton, not coincidentally, limned in an article for the magazine *Outlook*.

This Cincinnatus strategy was the wisest course available, for Coolidge couldn't have won outright. Despite his folk-hero status, not even his own Massachusetts delegation united behind his candidacy. Henry Cabot Lodge, for one, had grown cool toward the governor because Coolidge's ally Murray Crane was trying to get the GOP to defy Lodge and support the League of Nations. (Lodge was also loyal to his friend General Leonard Wood, the U.S. Army chief of staff, one of the leading contenders for the nomination.) In any event, Coolidge's failure to hold his own state deterred other delegations from offering him their full-throated backing.

Nonetheless, the governor's men, operating out of Morrow's hotel suite, worked the convention. (Coolidge himself, as was the custom then, didn't attend.) Barton distributed copies of a new book of Coolidge speeches on the day's hottest issue, called *Law and Order*. Coolidge's nomination drew some notice for being seconded by a woman, the actress Alexandra Carlisle—a historic first for a second. But the mention of his name sparked only a brief floor demonstration, compared to displays of half an hour or more for Wood, for Illinois governor Frank Lowden, and for California senator Hiram Johnson. On the opening ballots, Coolidge netted a mere handful of votes.

For eight rounds, Lowden and Wood duked it out. Suddenly, on the ninth ballot—thanks to some now-storied horse trading in the "smoke-filled rooms" on the thirteenth floor of the Blackstone Hotel—the handsome if undistinguished Senator Warren Harding of Ohio emerged as the leader in votes. After a bit of deft politicking from his manager, Harry Daugherty, Harding won the nomination on the tenth ballot. Coolidge received the news in Boston, where Grace had joined him. Upon hearing it, he donned his hat, left the Adams House, and walked alone across the common and through the city streets to cope with his disappointment.

Back in Chicago, attention turned to the vice-presidential nomination, also an open contest. Wisconsin senator Irvine Lenroot emerged as the favorite of the Senate Old Guard bosses, who had settled on Harding's nomination and wanted to balance the conservative Ohioan with a liberal. But many delegates had gone home after the presidential contest, and Coolidge's name remained in the air as a contender for the number-two spot. As the roll call began, delegates balked at having this choice imposed by fiat as well. Voices from the floor called out Coolidge's name; the Oregon delegation formally nominated him; and a stampede began for the Massachusetts governor. Supporters whipped out the "law and order" banners that they had stashed under their seats after his halfhearted presidential bid. Coolidge won the understudy spot easily, 674½ votes to 146½ for Lenroot, on the first ballot.

Coolidge was back at the Adams House when his phone rang.

After a short exchange, he hung up and reported to Grace with typical terseness, "Nominated for vice president."

"You aren't going to take it, are you?" she asked, knowing his dismay over having lost the big prize, and the obscurity with which most vice presidents eventually met.

"I suppose I shall have to," he replied. His sobriety masked an inner satisfaction. In ten minutes, friends and reporters were at the door, pressing him for comment. Sitting sphinxlike, he savored a cigar.

• • •

The fall campaign was a rout. Disillusioned with Wilson's ambitious agenda, most voters nodded in agreement when Harding promised a return to "normalcy," even as his ungainly coinage made grammarians wince. Barton, along with the advertising man Albert Lasker and the future motion picture czar Will Hays, applied the new art of public relations to the task of electing Harding and Coolidge. Wishing to evoke the fondly remembered William McKinley and his 1896 victory, they had Harding wage a "front porch" campaign from his hometown of Marion, Ohio, hauling a flagpole across north-central Ohio from McKinley's native Canton. Coolidge did the stumping. He toured the Northeast and reluctantly made a foray into the Democratic South, sounding his themes of thrift, industry, and common sense in government. Newsreels played up his rural roots, showing him splitting wood and hacking tall grass with a scythe on his father's farm. Meanwhile, on the Democratic side, Ohio governor James Cox and his running mate, the young assistant secretary of the navy, Franklin Delano Roosevelt, followed Wilson's lead and focused excessively on the Republicans' efforts to straddle the League of Nations question—thus calling undue attention to their own pro-League stand, which lacked the resounding popular support they imagined.[15]

November 2, Harding's fifty-fifth birthday, was Election Day. The returns, broadcast nationally on radio for the first time, offered a special thrill but no great surprises. The Republicans swept the country except the South, garnering 60 percent of the popular vote nationally and 404 of the 531 electoral votes. "The radicalism which had tinged our whole political and economic life from soon after 1900 to the World War period was passed," Coolidge said. He called it "the end of a period which has seemed to substitute words for things."[16]

Although the office of vice president held no great allure, Coolidge later realized he had been fortunate to have won that spot and not the presidency. "I am not gifted with intuition," he wrote. "I need not only hard work but experience to solve problems." Besides, he noted, "The Presidents who have gone to Washington without first having held some national office have been at great disadvantage." Biding his time as lieutenant governor had served him well in his quest for the governor's chair. Serving dutifully as vice president might well do the same.[17]

In the 1920s the vice presidency was little more than a ceremonial office whose chief duty was to preside over the Senate, and Calvin Coolidge did not expand its boundaries. Harding had promised him a role in the government and, in a historic move, allowed his vice president to join cabinet meetings. But Coolidge didn't participate much. "Aside from speeches, I did little writing," he recalled of those years, "but I read a great deal and listened much. While I little realized it at the time, it was for me a period of most important preparation." Slowly, Coolidge grew acclimated to the Washington landscape.[18]

The government lacked a residence for the vice president, so Coolidge continued to rent a hotel suite. With their sons, now teenagers, at boarding school in Pennsylvania, the vice president and his wife lived in a four-room apartment at the Willard Hotel in downtown Washington. Still a relatively friendless figure, Coolidge passed his time attending social functions. Although he was capable of enjoying the rounds of dinners and parties, he just as often endured them. ("Got to eat somewhere," he snorted when asked about his frequent dining out.) Grace, in contrast, easily slipped into the role of society woman. "She had a simplicity and charm," commented Alice Roosevelt Longworth, the daughter of Theodore Roosevelt and a doyenne of the Washington scene, " . . . amused by all the official functions and attentions, yet as always absolutely natural and unimpressed by it all."[19]

More important to the vice president were the speeches he gave. He was, he wrote Stearns, "loaded up with speeches, working from early morning until late in the night." His favorite were his rhapsodies about the splendors of the American past, but he also delivered more substantive remarks that showed a growing conservatism. In 1921 he put his name to a series of magazine articles entitled "Enemies of the Republic" that warned of Communist ideas taking hold among students, though their stridency, uncharacteristic of Coolidge, raises the possibility that Barton or another ghostwriter authored the pieces.[20]

On the whole, Coolidge wasn't much of a force in politics, the capital, or the nation. The Harding administration concerned itself with pushing for tax cuts, but even on an issue so dear to his heart, Coolidge wasn't deeply involved. Nor did he play a large role in the passage of the 1921 Budget and Accounting Act, the most important law enacted under Harding. Other changes, too, were afoot in the early 1920s. The nation was converting from a wartime to a peacetime economy, riding out the short but painful depression of 1921. In the wake of World War I, the country was engaged in a vigorous debate over arms control, and Harding hosted a celebrated conference in Washington. Radios and automobiles were changing everyday life. Coolidge spoke prominently on none of these issues.

His obscurity, in fact, became something of a joke. Complimentary baseball passes issued by the American and National Leagues printed his name with middle initials he didn't possess. A popular 1921 book of political gossip profiled Harding, Wilson, Lodge, and others but omitted him. Even around town, he went unrecognized. When the Willard was evacuated after a fire, a marshal stopped Coolidge from heading back to his suite.

"I'm the vice president," Coolidge insisted.

The marshal let him proceed at first but then reconsidered. "What are you vice president of?"

"I am the vice president of the United States," came the indignant reply.

"Come right down," said the marshal. "I thought you were vice president of the hotel."[21]

Again, political observers concluded that Coolidge was an unremarkable man who had risen as high as he was going to rise. Again, they were mistaken.

3

The New President

On August 2, 1923, on a summer tour of the West, President Warren Harding was seized by a massive fatal heart attack in his San
Francisco hotel room.[1] His sudden death unleashed shock and grief
as the news spread around the country. Though remembered today
as unremarkable or worse, Harding was at the time beloved: good-
looking, genial, and well liked, he conveyed a sense of ease and fun
that proved a welcome relief from the earnest Woodrow Wilson.
What was more, few Americans yet knew about the scandals that
would soon tarnish his name; many, including Coolidge, admired
his achievements. "It would be difficult to find two years of peacetime history in all of our republic that were marked with more
important and far-reaching accomplishments," Coolidge maintained,
citing higher tariffs, lower taxes, the new budget system, and the
postwar peace that Harding had struck with the Central Powers.[2]

While much of the country mourned, in Plymouth Notch the
reaction was one of awe. On the night of August 2, Coolidge was
visiting his father, still tending his farm at age seventy-eight, who
after midnight answered a sharp rap at the front door of the white
two-story cottage where he had raised his son. Receiving the news
of Harding's death from the owner of the nearest telephone
exchange—the "farmer's line" at his 250-year-old house wasn't
equipped to handle long-distance calls—John Coolidge climbed
the stairs, his voice quavering as he called his son's name. "As the

only time I had ever observed that before was when death had visited our family," his son recalled, "I knew that something of the gravest nature had occurred."[3]

Emotion flooded the new president. As he recounted it, he remembered the devotion his father had shown toward him over the years—ferrying him over mountain passes to his prep school in winter storms—"in the hope that I might sometime rise to a position of importance." For his father to be the first to recognize him as the new president invested the moment with special poignancy. Coolidge dressed, knelt, said a prayer, and went downstairs. "I believe I can swing it," he recalled thinking, betraying his familiar blend of modesty and self-confidence.[4]

Soon the house was abuzz. From nearby Bridgewater, a stenographer sped over. From Ludlow, the reporters traveling with the vice president hurried up to Plymouth. The cacophony of their sputtering cars on the hilly roads woke the neighbors. Lamplights flecked the Vermont night. Once the newspapermen arrived, the new president issued a statement. He said he would continue Harding's policies and keep his cabinet. Intuitively, he realized that the tenor of his presidency should stay true to Harding's theme of normalcy.

The men at the house found a copy of the Constitution in John Coolidge's library. They typed up the oath of office and gave it to the elder Coolidge, who as a notary public was deemed capable of administering it to his son.* Then, in the small downstairs parlor, by the glow of a kerosene lamp, a small group gathered that included the local newspaper editor, Coolidge's assistant, his chauffeur, and his wife. The new president, his face pale, his mother's Bible on the table, somberly recited the thirty-five-word oath. The clock on the mantel read 2:47 A.M.[5]

---

*Attorney General Harry Daugherty, a Harding crony, raised questions about whether a state official could administer the oath, and so Coolidge would repeat the ceremony two weeks later with a federal judge in Washington. The vice president by law need not take any oath to succeed to the office. He becomes president automatically when the president dies.

Had Coolidge planned this chain of events, he could not have devised more propitious atmospherics. The spare rural scene exuded the New England virtues of simplicity, piety, and duty on which he traded. Upon returning to Washington, Coolidge further burnished the image of the common man thrust into the seat of power. He dined with Florence Harding and insisted on staying in the Willard while she vacated the White House. Although Coolidge had been attending Washington's First Congregational Church, he now saw fit to formally join it. On August 5, he accepted the offer from the Reverend Jason Pierce, the minister and a fellow Amherst man, to take communion. Attendance at Sunday services multiplied as a result, and Edmund Starling would issue a report urging the church to reinforce its rickety balconies to accommodate the swelling congregation.[6]

Coolidge also ingratiated himself with the White House press corps. At his first full press conference, on August 14, the president pledged to the 150 reporters huddled around him to continue Harding's twice-weekly sessions and to always be available. The correspondents in turn sized him up, the *New York Times* wrote, as "frankly spoken, affable, and courteous." Afterward, he gamely posed with them for the photographers. When one of the motion picture cameramen suggested three cheers for the new president, Coolidge spared the reporters an awkward moment by insisting diplomatically, "This [hurrah] also includes the opposition." A hearty ovation followed, which the president recalled as a highlight of his presidency.[7]

These moves spoke to the hard work and savvy that Coolidge showed in his first months in office as he sought the legitimacy that every vice president who inherits the top office has to struggle to attain. Initially, there were doubters. When Henry Cabot Lodge heard that Harding had died, he exclaimed, "My God! That means Coolidge is president!" Others took an equally dim view. Coolidge could "no more run this big machine at Washington," sniped Senator Peter Norbeck of South Dakota, "than could a paralytic." Added Harold Ickes, a Theodore Roosevelt progressive: "If this country has reached the state where Coolidge is the right sort of a person for president, then any office boy is qualified to be chief executive."[8]

Pundits, too, belittled Coolidge. They described him as inveterately lucky, somehow always at the right place at the right time. A popular joke cast him as a baseball player who reached first base on a walk, stole second base, got to third on an error, and reached home because the catcher died. Even people who knew him well and admired him didn't necessarily think him presidential material. "A lot of people in Plymouth can't understand how I got to be president," Coolidge told the journalist William Allen White, "least of all my father."[9]

In less than a year, however, Coolidge would silence many of his doubters. Writers and wits still disparaged his abilities and railed against his conservatism. But Coolidge managed several feats soon after taking office. He contained, after initial missteps, the burgeoning scandals that would posthumously tar Harding's legacy. He set a political agenda that, despite his troubles pushing it through Congress, helped define his era. And, for all his political errors in dealing with Capitol Hill, he mastered the new politics of public opinion, emerging as a hugely popular politician associated with the decade's economic surge. In time, this cautious, unassuming Vermonter would come to embody the virtues of probity and moderation at a time of cultural ferment, of dutifulness and thrift in an era of irresponsibility and exploding consumer capitalism.

. . .

The 1920s have usually been portrayed as a time of resurgent conservatism after two decades of progressivism, with Warren Harding, Calvin Coolidge, and Herbert Hoover constituting a triumvirate of Republican restorers. "After the World War the reaction in American social and political thinking snapped back beyond Wilsonian idealism," wrote William Allen White, "back even beyond Taft's chuckling laissez-faire complacence, back of Roosevelt to the Hanna period that followed the Spanish-American War and its rising imperialism."[10]

As White surely knew, that simple pendulum's arc traces too neat a path. While the Republican ascendancy of the 1920s certainly signaled a muting of progressive impulses, more dissonance and dissent roiled Washington than the trifecta of Republican presidential victories would suggest. In the 1922 midterm elections, for example, the Democrats made huge gains in both houses of Congress. Though they failed to win majorities, their victories shattered the solid support on Capitol Hill that Harding had enjoyed on taking office. These off-year gains—and the seats the Democrats would pick up in the 1926 congressional elections—were not tantamount to holding the White House, but they did keep Coolidge from being able to work his will on the Hill.

Coolidge also faced opposition on some issues from within his own party, which was far from unified. Ever since Theodore Roosevelt had bolted the GOP to run for president on his Bull Moose ticket in 1912, the Republicans had been divided. The "Old Guard" against whom Roosevelt had rebelled remained staunchly right wing and allied with business. In contrast, some of Roosevelt's followers, while making peace with these party stalwarts, retained a strain of liberal noblesse oblige and a commitment to internationalism in foreign policy that tempered their conservatism. Still others— the so-called farm bloc of westerners—claimed Roosevelt's progressive label, though they were cut of different ideological cloth. With their constituents facing persistent hard times, such progressive senators from the western and Great Plains states as William Borah, Hiram Johnson, Robert La Follette, George Norris, and Burton Wheeler—many of them holding powerful positions on Senate committees—kept an insurgent spirit alive. Thus, conservatives may have dominated the scene, but America remained divided.

Coolidge fit uneasily into this puzzle. Even within his own party he occupied no clear niche. "He is not easy to classify as either a Conservative or a Progressive—the two major lines of political division," noted Bascom Slemp, the conservative Virginia congressman whom Coolidge hired as his chief aide. With his northeastern breeding, his exaltation of character, and his view of public service as ennobling, Coolidge was probably closest in type to elite Rooseveltians such as Henry Cabot Lodge, Elihu Root, and Henry Stimson.

And yet his small-town roots and mind-set, so fundamental to his politics, made him an altogether different creature from these well-born internationalists. Most telling of all, he was said privately to despise Theodore Roosevelt. Similarly, despite his sporadic liberal tendencies, Coolidge was not one of the 1920s progressives. He lacked the requisite affection for activist government and visceral contempt for plutocracy. Finally, while he shared the Old Guard's esteem for business and small government, Coolidge was never really one of their number either. During the Harding years, the heyday of the Old Guard's restoration, Coolidge had remained aloof and alienated. Besides, in terms of personal style, Coolidge was as different from Harding "as a New England front parlor is from a back room in a speakeasy," in the words of Alice Roosevelt Longworth.[11]

Still, on becoming president Coolidge saw little reason to tinker with Harding's formula. He kept his predecessor's cabinet, as promised, including the energetic Herbert Hoover at Commerce, the haughty Andrew Mellon at Treasury, and the pragmatic Charles Evans Hughes at State. On the whole he stayed true to their agendas—most enthusiastically to Mellon's program of tax and budget cutting that the Treasury secretary would seek to advance regularly for the rest of the decade.

A less trumpeted but important decision was to retain Judson Welliver, a former newspaperman who worked for Harding as "literary clerk." In effect, Welliver served as a White House publicity man and the first dedicated presidential speechwriter. (It was Welliver who coined the phrase "Founding Fathers," though Harding often received the credit.) Under Coolidge Welliver earned a handsome salary of $7,500, equal to that of senior aides. Although Coolidge worked hard on his own speeches and wrote far more of them than had Harding, Welliver learned to ape the new president's style as ably as he had mimicked his predecessor's. Indeed, said H. L. Mencken, he made Coolidge's style "simpler and clearer," though he added, "It continued to be, in essence, a device for flabbergasting newspaper editorial writers without actually saying anything . . . to roar like a hurricane without letting loose any compromising ideas." Coolidge's retention of Welliver—and his decision to preserve the post upon Welliver's departure in 1925 by replacing him with Stuart Crawford, another Amherst classmate—signaled how important press aides were becoming to the presidency.[12]

Every president, of course, needs a few trusted aides at his side, and Coolidge made a few key appointments of his own. Though his old mentor Murray Crane had died in 1920, William Butler and Frank Stearns from Massachusetts were on hand for counsel; Coolidge came to view Stearns, a frequent dinner companion, as playing the *consigliere* role that Colonel Edward House had for Wilson. There was talk of appointing Bruce Barton secretary to the president, but Coolidge chose instead Slemp, who had allies on Capitol Hill and at the Republican National Committee. These hires, however, scarcely signaled a break from Harding's direction. Normalcy would continue.

· · ·

There was one area in which a break with the Harding administration was not just wise but necessary. When Harding died, the Teapot Dome scandal, as it came to be called, was just starting to claim the president's attention. Harding himself was not venal, but he had a weakness for placing unscrupulous men in his cabinet. "I have no trouble with my enemies," he once remarked, ". . . but my damn friends . . . my goddamn friends . . . they're the ones that keep me walking the floor nights!"[13]

Even while Harding was still alive, news was surfacing about several corrupt transactions involving his aides. The most sweeping centered on Secretary of the Interior Albert Fall's giveaway of federal oil reserves—at Teapot Dome, Wyoming, and Elk Hills, California—to two businessmen in exchange for large sums of money. Fall and one of the oil moguls, Harry Sinclair, would eventually serve prison time for the shady deal, while two other cabinet members—Secretary of the Navy Edwin Denby and Postmaster General Will Hays would suffer taint. Separate scandals would implicate the director of the veterans bureau, Charles Forbes, and the late president's crony Harry Daugherty, whom Harding had foolishly installed as attorney general.

Like Watergate in its day, Teapot Dome came to denote the whole raft of Harding scandals, which were seen as outgrowths of the president's penchant for surrounding himself with morally challenged men. The first to break had been the veterans scandal, in 1922. It was a case of pure graft: Forbes had arranged with contractors to build outrageously overpriced hospitals, stocked with outrageously overpriced goods ($70,000 for floor wax and cleaner), which the government then sold at fire-sale prices. Forbes pocketed kickbacks. Here Harding had acted diligently, firing Forbes in early 1923. Other cases of venality, however, passed the president without notice or even with his unwitting participation. Egregiously, in the case of Teapot Dome, Harding signed off on the transfer of the government oil reserves from the U.S. Navy to the Interior Department that enabled Secretary Fall to line his pockets in the first place.

It fell to Coolidge to clean up the mess. In the autumn of 1923, as the new president was just getting his bearings, the Senate began investigating both the Forbes affair and the early reports about Teapot Dome. Led by Wisconsin's "Fighting Bob" La Follette and Montana Democrat Thomas Walsh, the progressive coalition spearheaded the probe. Though no doubt sincerely troubled by the corruption, they plainly had political motives as well, and many observers at first viewed the investigations as routine political harassment. Newspaper editorials labeled the senators "scandal-mongers," "mud-gunners," and "assassins of character"—even after the facts had justified their inquiries.[14]

By the new year, however, disclosures were mounting high enough to inflame the public. In January 1924, the oilman Edward Doheny told a Senate hearing that he had given Albert Fall $100,000 in a little black bag. Harry Sinclair also confessed to giving bonds to the Interior secretary. Fall claimed the Fifth Amendment. With the facts looking grim, the Republican National Committee sought to discredit the investigations by accusing Senator Walsh and others of Bolshevik sympathies. But the smear job had limited results. Far vaster in scope than Forbes's payola scheme, Teapot Dome not only surpassed its sister scandal in magnitude but outstripped past imbroglios, including the Grant administration's 1872 Crédit Mobilier affair, as the benchmark for presidential wrongdoing. Not until Watergate would it be surpassed.

Coolidge temporized. Vowing to enforce the law, he pledged to appoint a special prosecutor from each party to probe the case. Yet even as he faced a barrage of questions about the scandals at his press conferences, he didn't grasp their gravity; playing for time, the president said he wouldn't personally "determine criminal guilt or render judgment in civil cases." Making matters worse, his first choices for the special prosecutor job both turned out to have oil industry ties and aroused Senate opposition. Withdrawing their names, Coolidge instead chose former senator Atlee Pomerene and future Supreme Court justice Owen Roberts.[15]

As the winter of 1923–24 wore on, the president remained protective of the Harding gang. His sense of duty to fulfill his predecessor's agenda overrode his better judgment. When in late January the Senate demanded that the president dismiss Navy Secretary Edwin Denby—for having agreed to transfer the oil reserves from his department to Fall's—the president balked. Several days later, however, Denby resigned on his own, rendering Coolidge's passivity moot. Nonetheless Coolidge showed his sympathies, telling Denby, "You will go with the knowledge that your honesty and integrity have not been impugned." In fact, the opposite was true: Denby's reputation would suffer, although historians have judged him to have been more dupe than scoundrel.[16]

There was more to come. Still another member of Harding's cabinet was running into trouble: Attorney General Harry Daugherty, the late president's closest associate. A classic hack, Daugherty was unconcerned about policy and ethically lax. His problem was twofold. First, questions arose about whether he had tried to block the Teapot Dome investigation; second, it came to light that he may have received bribes himself. A friend and associate of Daugherty's,

Jess Smith, had helped a group of German bankers recoup $7 billion in securities they claimed to have lost in the world war. After receiving a $224,000 kickback from the deal, Smith placed a chunk of his ill-gotten gains in an account he shared with the attorney general. The Senate, its investigative machinery already up and running, set to work.

Like Denby, Daugherty would never be convicted of a crime. With the odor of scandal around him, however, he too became a liability. (Smith committed suicide.) But rather than jettisoning Daugherty, Coolidge bizarrely summoned him to the White House to meet with himself and Borah, one of Daugherty's chief critics, as if he were mediating a personal feud. "Don't let my presence embarrass you," Daugherty sneered at Borah, who was surprised to have to lobby the president for the attorney general's ouster in his presence. "I think I should be the least embarrassed person here," Borah retorted. A shouting match ensued; Coolidge puffed a cigar. Ultimately, the senator prevailed. Daugherty marched noisily out of the White House in an incandescent rage. Still, he refused to resign, and Coolidge was left with no choice but to fire him. On March 27, he finally did.[17]

Although the scandals were Harding's, not Coolidge's, they could easily have tripped up the new president, especially given his early errors. Many observers, especially Democrats, expected the daily banner headlines to spell doom for the Republicans in 1924. But as in the Boston police strike, Coolidge recovered from his missteps and insulated himself from the fallout. In June, his special counsels called for the prosecution of Fall, Sinclair, and Doheny, as well as of Doheny's son, who had ferried the "little black bag" of money to Fall. The public accepted that justice was being done, just as the scandals were growing too baroque to sustain newspaper readers' attention. "COOLIDGE HITS OIL DEALS!" a *Washington Times* headline read. "Has quietly assumed control of the situation—Surprise awaits his foes."[18]

Coolidge's air of rectitude aided his recovery. By dispatching the worst of the Ohio Gang, however halfheartedly, he unloaded an albatross. His own upstanding appointees to the cabinet—California judge Curtis Wilbur at Navy; former Columbia University law school dean Harlan Fiske Stone at Justice—enhanced his aura of integrity. Coolidge also fired William Burns, the head of the Federal Bureau of Investigation, who was implicated in the scandals, replacing him with a young man with a reputation for honesty, J. Edgar Hoover. A housecleaning at the Republican National Committee allowed Coolidge to move his own allies, notably William Butler, into power there. And since the Senate investigations found no wrongdoing by Coolidge himself, his personal reputation emerged enhanced. Even the president's boilerplate about not prejudging the cases had gone over well.

In contrast to the stench of the Harding pols, Coolidge seemed a breath of fresh Vermont air. Here was the germ of the public persona that William Allen White would later call, in the title of his biography, the Puritan in Babylon. Coolidge reassured the swelling ranks of middle-class Americans who, Walter Lippmann observed, "can [now] afford luxury and are buying it furiously, largely on the installment plan." As Lippmann explained, these New Era consumers could tell themselves that they "are stern, ascetic and devoted to plain living because they vote for a man who is."[19]

Lippmann came close to capturing Coolidge's appeal, but he missed one important aspect of it. While Coolidge's morality and old-fashioned values reassured a public concerned about the erosion of personal virtue, the president was no crusading ideologue seeking to turn back the clock. Rather, his parsimony, his modesty, and his preachments about small government seemed to demonstrate that these values could thrive in a contemporary environment. He did not deplore corporate capitalism, or technology, or even consumer spending; he accepted these elements of modernity while trusting in his religious faith and staying vigilant against moral decay. By his example, he gave hope that the mores of the old century might yet survive in the new one.

4

Hitting His Stride

Calvin Coolidge's air of rectitude comforted Americans in a time of shifting values. It helped him to navigate the shoals of the Harding scandals and, later, to rally the public when his legislative leadership proved weak. Indeed, the quirks and habits that made up the Silent Cal persona invested Coolidge's tenure in office with much of its distinctive flavor.

A neglected element of Coolidge's appeal was his religiosity, which was both genuine and generic, pervasive and personal. Coolidge took office at a time when the public culture of the United States was becoming more secular, and the president's bland piety affirmed a central place for faith in American culture without triggering fears of the kind of moral crusade associated with the Ku Klux Klan or fundamentalist anti-Darwinism. Sincerely devout, Coolidge believed unquestioningly in the Protestant values with which he was raised, though he showed no signs of having thought much about theology. His was a soft spiritualism, bearing the imprint of his college professor Charles Garman and sharing affinities with the "social gospel" that liberal Protestants of the day espoused—albeit without the robust liberal politics that often accompanied it. "Our government rests upon religion," Coolidge said in 1924. "It is from that source that we derive our reverence for truth and justice, for equality and liberty, and for the rights of mankind." And though the president quoted often from the Bible in his speeches, he never deployed Christian teachings as a political weapon. He described himself as "an instrument in the hands of God"—not to suggest grandiosely that a divinity had selected him for leadership but to underscore what he called his "increasing sense of humility" at having "been placed in the White House."[1]

Just as his religion was mostly unreflective, so was his interest in history, which he studied mainly to buttress his homiletic and patriotic speeches. A speech he delivered at the Jewish Community Center of Washington, for example—which must have required significant research—included an admiring but dry and potted history of Jews in America, teeming with antiquarian tidbits about the influence of Mosaic law on the legal code of Connecticut and about "Hebrews" who served in the Revolutionary army. Admirable for its strong defense of toleration, it lacked much in the way of analysis.[2]

Coolidge preferred experience to ratiocination and valued knowledge for practical, not intellectual, purposes. Although built-in bookshelves were installed in the White House to accommodate his voluminous library, Grace attested that he read little and that when he did he preferred books "with the object of 'improving the mind,' an expression he used often." The journalist Gamaliel Bradford suggested that Coolidge's references to books sounded "more like the respect of one who reveres afar off than with any intimate daily acquaintance." This anti-intellectual tenor pervaded Coolidge's presidency.[3]

An impatience with what Coolidge considered needless complexities contributed, somewhat unfairly, to his reputation for slacking in office. Ike Hoover, the head White House usher, claimed that Coolidge worked less than any other president he had known. But Coolidge's schedule wasn't lax. Never an athlete, he maintained his lifelong trimness by starting his day with a morning constitutional, on which Starling accompanied him. After breakfast, usually with Grace, Coolidge began holding meetings by 9 A.M. and continued through the morning. In the afternoon, he would greet droves of White House tourists—he was the last president to work the rope lines regularly—and once shook hands with 1,900 callers in 34 minutes, probably a record. In early afternoon Coolidge took a nap, the duration of which became a source of some contention: Coolidge claimed his naps lasted one hour, Ike Hoover said "two to four hours," and his biographer Claude Fuess, splitting the difference, settled on two. Afternoons were spent immersed in the pile of documents that invariably awaited, with no more than one or two appointments scheduled. Sometimes Coolidge would find time for more exercise, on a mechanical hobbyhorse he purchased—to titters in the press corps—or on what he described cryptically in his memoirs as "the vibrating machines kept in my room." The Coolidges typically dined as a couple, with Frank Stearns and his wife sometimes joining them as well.[4]

How much Coolidge worked at night is hard to determine. He claimed that after dinner he drafted speeches and messages and retired by ten o'clock. But Starling recalled the president saying explicitly that he didn't work at night, and that a man who couldn't finish his tasks during the daytime couldn't be terribly smart. Certainly, the president passed more than a few evenings in a rocking chair on the White House portico, smoking a cigar—though eventually the crowds that flocked to watch drove him indoors or to the back porch. Either way, Coolidge became known publicly for going to bed early. Once, when he attended the live Marx Brothers revue *Animal Crackers*—later the classic movie—Groucho spied the president in the audience and from the stage quipped: "Isn't it past your bedtime, Calvin?"[5]

Political writers remarked on habits like Coolidge's early bedtime because they evoked a lost age—the old order of the New England village, the slower pace of rural America. And in many ways Coolidge had never left Plymouth Notch. Disdainful of packaged foods, he had the White House cook whip up a morning cereal by boiling raw wheat and rye, which he sometimes ate while having his scalp massaged with Vaseline. He shaved with a straight razor, even though safety razors had been around for decades. A formal man, he rarely called colleagues by their first names, not even friends such as "Mr. Butler" or "Mr. Stearns" (though by one account

"Mr. Morrow" was sometimes graced with "Dwight"), and in speaking to others he would refer to "Ol' Man Stearns" or "Ol' Andy Mellon." Disliking travel, he never ventured outside the United States, apart from a brief honeymoon in Montreal and a 1928 diplomatic trip to Havana. "I have so many places to go in the United States that I don't know when . . . I will arrive at a time when I can visit other countries," he once said. He never did.[6]

Nonetheless, Coolidge wasn't immune to the charm of modern amusements. For relaxation and solitude, he repaired to the presidential yacht, the *Mayflower*, after Sunday church services. Like millions of Americans, he became a movie buff—"the first national executive to depend on motion pictures," *Film Classic* reported, "as his sole recreation." He screened films on the yacht, on his vacations, and in the White House, once with a forty-four-piece orchestra brought down from New York. On a post-presidential journey to Los Angeles, he visited the MGM studios, where he watched as the filming of a Ramon Novarro film was disrupted by a rampaging trained bear, leading Coolidge to break out in uncharacteristic hysterics.[7]

There was a boyish simplicity to Coolidge that was all the more winning because of his usual dourness. He amused himself by bestowing nicknames on the White House staff—John Mays, a doorman, was "The Mink," and the butler, named Thomas Roach, was "Bug"—though many saw this trait as condescending or cruel. Likewise, the practical jokes for which Coolidge was known were, to different observers, either appealingly childish or gratuitously nasty. He would ring the White House doorbell and then hide behind the curtains, or press the buzzer to announce his impending arrival at the White House, only to head out the door for a stroll as staffers scurried around to prepare for him. "Anyone who cannot revert to boyhood in a big job is lost," said Coolidge's White House physician, James Coupal. "That's just what Calvin Coolidge did. He was always kidding." The president agreed. "Do you know," he once said to Stearns, "I've never really grown up?"[8]

Coolidge's attitude toward his wife also smacked of an earlier time. Feminism was in full flower in the 1920s. Women had just secured a constitutional amendment giving them the vote, and the nation was becoming comfortable with powerful women as first ladies. Edith Wilson had all but served as president after her husband's hushed-up stroke of 1919, and Florence Harding was immersed in her husband's affairs—at least the professional ones. Grace Coolidge, moreover, was an educated, modern woman. But the president shut her out of his political business. She barely knew the members of his cabinet and was often clueless about his schedule; once, when she asked for it, he replied, "Grace, we don't give that information out promiscuously"—his sarcasm failing to conceal the underlying contempt. Considering himself the head of the household, he supervised his wife's spending, second-guessed her social plans, and occasionally acted with unbecoming nastiness. Sometimes he refused to talk to her for days. Grace grew irritated at his treatment and early in their marriage wondered if she could remain with him forever. But for all his chauvinism, he clearly loved her, and when she was away—hating Washington's humid climate, she often withdrew to Northampton—he would sort through the White House mail to cull the letters she sent him, stuffing them in his pocket to read in private. The devotion was touching, particularly in a man whose losses had led him to shield his vulnerabilities.[9]

The curtness with which Coolidge often treated Grace—and the sternness remembered by his sons—was characteristic. He could be prickly and impatient, and Ike Hoover wrote that White House employees lived in "fear and trembling, lest they lose their jobs . . . [Coolidge] kept them in a state of constant anxiety" with his outbursts. Even admirers such as Starling attested to the president's short temper. Once, after a fishing outing on which the agent caught more fish than the president, Coolidge angrily insisted they return home at once, refusing to wait for Starling even to dismantle the rods, and, upon arriving at his hotel, "walked through the crowd in the lobby without speaking or looking to left or right, got in the elevator and went up to his room."[10]

Coolidge's anger was mostly kept private, however, whereas his endearing eccentricities were evident to the public. He made the most of his old-fashioned ways, allowing his personality and private habits to become fodder for news stories. "I think the American public wants a solemn ass as a president," he quipped to the actress Ethel Barrymore, "and I think I'll go along with them."[11]

. . .

The restraint that marked Coolidge's private behavior also colored his political style. Uninterested in the minutiae of policy, he didn't think that consulting a bevy of experts would help him solve problems and preferred to work alone. He was often seen in the White House, as Slemp put it, "thinking and thinking and thinking." Coolidge saw the presidency as a position of isolation, its burdens to be borne dutifully.[12]

Accordingly, the president delegated most official business. "He is not so much an originator of policy as a policy administrator," said Slemp. As governor during the police strike, he had deferred to the judgment of Commissioner Curtis; as president, he assigned decisions to agency heads. This practice fed the impression that he was a slacker and meant that others often got credit or blame for the president's policies: Attorney General Harlan Fiske Stone shared the plaudits for restoring integrity to the Justice Department after the Harding scandals; Ambassador Dwight Morrow won praise for his diplomacy in Mexico in 1927; and Secretary of Commerce Herbert Hoover drew the acclaim for delivering relief after the 1927 Mississippi flood. Yet Coolidge believed his hands-off approach freed him to focus on his duties. For those problems that demanded presidential attention, there too he deemed inaction the better part of efficiency. "If you see ten troubles coming down the road," Coolidge would advise Hoover, "you can be sure that nine will run into the ditch before they reach you, and you have to battle with only one of them."[13]

For all its virtues, there was a shortsightedness to Coolidge's preference for letting problems pass—not least because they sometimes didn't. This wait-and-see approach prevented Coolidge from pursuing the kinds of goals that can make presidents great. In keeping with the norms of his day, he didn't feel a need to propose any grand vision or goals—even though Theodore Roosevelt and Woodrow Wilson had risen above the prevailing expectations for the office to do so. "Both Mr. Roosevelt and Mr. Wilson cherished visions of a better America," noted the *New Republic* in December 1923. "But Mr. Coolidge has not seen the vision of an America better than the America of which he is president." Coolidge probably wouldn't have minded the criticism. The nation had enough laws and regulations, he liked to say, and didn't need any more.[14]

Yet if Coolidge rejected his predecessors' activism, he followed their lead in his style of public leadership. He grasped that the growth of a mass industrial society and new forms of technology were changing politics. Traditionally, presidents had seldom appealed directly to the public through speeches or an independent press. Congress and party leaders had represented the people's concerns, with the president serving as an executive. But in the early twentieth century, as presidents assumed responsibility for setting the national agenda, they appealed increasingly to public opinion to do so. Reforms such as the secret ballot were limiting the influence of party bosses, while the rise of mass media, including film and radio, were making a politician's personality, rather than his party, central to his success. Where winning elections had once depended on the party mobilizing a large, loyal base of voters, it now relied on an individual's ability to rouse a broad range of citizens, including those willing to split their tickets.

Different competencies, therefore, were now required to succeed, and if Coolidge lacked the horse-trading talents of a legislative leader and the fine-grained feel for America's motley political cultures and voting blocs, he possessed the skills suited to the newer strategy of what the journalist William Allen White called going "over the heads of the politicians" and appealing directly to voters. He grasped how to use new tools of mass media and public relations to sell himself to America as a whole. "It is because in their hours of timidity the Congress becomes subservient to the importunities of organized minorities," Coolidge wrote, "that the president comes more and more to stand as the champion of the rights of the whole country." After turning the Harding scandals from a liability into an asset—a reminder of his own taut integrity—Coolidge continued to use his public persona as his chief political instrument.[15]

Coolidge accommodated himself to the demands of modern politics in part through the bully pulpit. "One of the most appalling trials which confront a president is the perpetual clamor for public utterances," Coolidge said. "Invitations are constant and pressing." Though he shuddered at the "attendant receptions," he met the challenge with hard work. "It requires the most laborious and extended research and study, and the most careful and painstaking thought. . . . It is not difficult for me to deliver an address. The difficulty lies in its preparation." But it was work Coolidge knew he could handle, and it allowed him to feel at ease behind the podium.[16]

Coolidge also "talked at length" to the newspapermen who covered the White House, according to Frederick Essary of the *Baltimore Sun*, a leading Washington correspondent. "He answered every question propounded and elaborately elucidated his answers," Essary recalled. "He was communicative to the point of garrulousness." More than most of his peers, Coolidge understood the press corps' growing importance, and his dedication to and skill at courting them—rated by some as equal to that of Theodore Roosevelt— remains an overlooked key to his success as president.[17]

Since at least the 1890s mass circulation newspapers—as opposed to the partisan broadsheets read by elites in earlier times— had been influencing national politics, and several of Coolidge's predecessors took strides toward integrating them into White House practice. But Coolidge's contributions were notable. As he had promised on taking office, he diligently met with reporters twice a week, on Tuesdays and Fridays, throughout his presidency. Wilson had started the regular parleys but abandoned them when he got fed up with the grilling. (His aide Joe Tumulty took over and fared much better.) Harding revived the conferences, but his two and a half years in office weren't enough to cement them as standard practice. Coolidge's commitment to a regular presidential press relationship entrenched the press conference as an official duty and, as a reporter wrote in 1927, "turned it into an engine for bringing himself almost daily into the American home." His use of the news corps underscored his determination to seek to reach the public above all, and not Congress, party leaders, or other rivals to presidential decision making.[18]

Coolidge tailored his sessions with reporters to his skills. He made them submit questions to him in writing so he could reply in an orderly fashion. He sometimes ignored a question for no reason besides his own whim, but reporters tolerated such exercises of his prerogative. He spoke "on background," meaning that the reporters could attribute his words to "a White House spokesman" but not to the president himself. The practice provoked grousing and mockery, and often the identity of this unnamed spokesman was so thinly disguised that any sentient newspaper reader would know it was the president and not some functionary offering his views. In one of the sharper critiques of Coolidge's ground rules, the political scientist Lindsay Rogers argued that the "White House 'spokesman' " amounted to "an extra-constitutional person who increases both presidential influence and irresponsibility." But the president defended the practice in terms consonant with his philosophy of reticence: "The words of the President have an enormous weight and ought not to be used indiscriminately. It would be exceedingly easy to set the country all by the ears and foment hatreds and jealousies, which, by destroying faith and confidence, would help nobody and harm everybody." Most reporters agreed that the shield, whatever its drawbacks, allowed the president to speak candidly. "At least I have some intimate close-up of what the president is thinking," explained Essary.[19]

Coolidge wasn't above flattering the correspondents. He once claimed (perhaps sarcastically) to be amazed "at the constant correctness of my views as you report them." He didn't pal around with reporters or flout Prohibition at card parties, as Harding had, but he did invite the journalists to dinners, social events, trips on the *Mayflower,* and even his summer vacations, earning their gratitude and goodwill. Newspaper moguls, too, including William Randolph Hearst and Clarence Barron of the *Wall Street Journal,* became social companions.[20]

Coolidge was equally sensitive to the needs of the newer corps of photographers and newsreel cameramen. "He avoided every appearance of publicity seeking, but he probably was the most photographed man who ever occupied the White House," noted Jay Hayden of the *Detroit News.* "It was a joke among the photographers that Mr. Coolidge would don any attire or assume any pose that would produce an interesting picture. He was never too busy to be photographed." Long before Ronald Reagan chopped wood at Santa Barbara or George W. Bush cleared sagebrush in Crawford, Coolidge's Plymouth Notch sojourns provided ideal settings to catch him working on the farm—however incongruous his black suit or dress shoes might appear. His aides were constantly communicating with professional photographers to take and print professional-quality portraits of the president.[21]

Coolidge also made avid use of newsreels. Theaters showed short films such as "Visitin' 'Round at Coolidge Corners"—more populist image making—before their features, reminding Americans of the president's rural roots. In April 1925, he became one of the first Americans to appear in a talking film. At a New York Friars Club dinner of some five hundred guests, Coolidge "spoke," the *New York Times* excitedly reported, "although the president was actually in Washington, more than 200 miles away." Less interested in the speech's message than its medium (then called the "phonofilm"), the *Times* reporter marveled, "The tones of his voice came clear and synchronized perfectly with the movement of his mouth. . . . Once during the speech the synchronization was so perfect that the guests gave involuntary applause." Lee De Forest, the phonofilm inventor, was so pleased that he took to using the short in demonstrations to attract investment in his machines, but Coolidge didn't like his words being used to drive up De Forest's company's stock. After an investigation by J. Edgar Hoover, the administration had De Forest desist. Taken aback, the filmmaker sent the reels to the White House, urging that they be donated to the Smithsonian Institution.[22]

The contrivance behind Coolidge's film appearances and photo ops didn't escape censure. Even in the 1920s critics bemoaned that image making was corrupting politics. "Certainly no president has ever been willing to submit to such nauseating exhibitions in the news reels as has Coolidge," noted Sherwin Cook, a political writer. "Cultured Americans wince at the thought of their president putting on a smock frock to pose while pitching hay and milking a bossy." Some White House aides feared their efforts would backfire. Ted Clark warned against disseminating one photograph of Coolidge in a rural setting because his formal "costume, while true to life on the farm at Plymouth, is . . . so different from any other that I doubt if the average farmer would believe it was real and not especially prepared for the occasion." The faux rural poses became a joke among reporters. At one Gridiron Dinner, they sang, to the tune of the Yale song "Boola Boola," "Mr. Coolidge went to Vermont upon a sunny day / The movies took his picture as he pitched the new-mown hay."[23]

Coolidge also endured rebukes for his efforts to shape the news. The most severe line of criticism suggested that he was undermining democracy with news management that hardened into propaganda. The rise of advertising and public relations, coupled with the odor left from Woodrow Wilson's barrage of propaganda to maintain support for the American war effort, left many people afraid that the public was becoming helpless to question how the government presented information. Ludwell Denny, a correspondent for the Scripps-Howard papers, called the press conferences "a vicious institution in American life [that] should be abolished"; he argued that Coolidge turned them into "propaganda agencies" and that "correspondents have to submit to protect themselves."[24]

On the whole, however, Coolidge's media-friendly strategy paid off—perhaps proving his critics' point. His obliging manner not only helped him choose the images that the public would see, it also endeared him to the men who conveyed those images to the public. Newspapermen conceded the positive tone of their coverage. "No president in our time has had such a 'good press,' " wrote the pseudonymous T.R.B. columnist in the *New Republic*. Though barbs still came from H. L. Mencken, for whom sourness was stock in trade, or from ideological critics such as Lincoln Steffens, among the workaday reporters Coolidge sustained steady favor. "Contrast what Mr. Wilson went through, in the shape of press criticism of his foreign policy, with the trivial nature of the Coolidge criticism," wrote Willis Sharp in the *Atlantic Monthly*. "I venture to say that neither in the domestic nor the foreign field has any president in this generation had as little as Mr. Coolidge—few have had less since the beginning."[25]

5

The Coolidge Prosperity

Calvin Coolidge's personal austerity provided the basis for his popularity, and his dexterity in handling the press boosted it. But it was the robust economic productivity of the times that kept him in public favor throughout his tenure. When Coolidge entered the White House in 1923, the nation had left behind the brief depression that had followed the end of World War I. The uncontrolled stock market speculation of the late 1920s remained a ways off, but the economy was beginning several years of solid growth, with minor interruptions, that would last until he left the White House. Pundits dubbed the boom the "Coolidge Prosperity."

Growth under Coolidge was uneven, to be sure. Recessions struck in 1924 and 1927, though they scarcely dampened the general optimism. Laborers in some sectors—textile workers, coal miners, and especially farmers—suffered badly. What was more, the maldistribution of wealth created instabilities in the economy that would have long-term consequences. But the prosperity was beginning to reach an enlarged middle class, and it appeared to bode well for increasingly widespread and long-lasting material comfort in the future. From 1923 to 1929, wages rose; inflation, unemployment, and interest rates fell. Coolidge kept the size of the overall federal budget more or less flat, at $3.3 billion, and cut the national debt by a quarter. Burgeoning tax receipts even allowed federal expenditures to show a net growth in the course of the decade. "This

period," observed George Soule, one of the most perceptive ana-
lysts of the era's economy, "was mainly characterized by a flowering
of what is commonly known as private enterprise, with a minimum
of governmental interference and a maximum of governmental
encouragement."[1]

Many observers, believing a fundamental shift had occurred,
hailed a "New Era." The turmoil of World War I and its aftermath
had given way, they argued, to a new set of economic relations.
Technology was raising wages and dispersing the ownership of capital, allowing a greater number of Americans to flourish economi-
cally. By mid-decade these gains were encouraging the conceit that
relatively unfettered capitalism had created the favorable conditions and that even looser fetters would multiply the propitious
outcomes. Even skeptics of this view—and critics of the Republican
policies that blessed it—felt security in knowing that the United
States had emerged from the tough times as the richest, most powerful country on earth. In what the poet Harry Crosby termed "the
Aerial Age," America seemed to be attaining unprecedented
heights, with towering skyscrapers, soaring aviators, and the con-
quest of the ether by radio embodying the idea that America had
reached a new level of civilization.[2]

The heady good times of the 1920s were rooted, ultimately, not
in Coolidge's policies but in the fortuitous economic state in which
the United States found itself after World War I. Military expenditures, which had underwritten much of the investment and productivity that emerged in the 1920s, were now greatly diminished.
Yet the seed money of wartime and the favorable amortization of
war plants continued to benefit American industry well into the
decade. Although the reduced military commitment created the
impression of a new budget efficiency under the Harding and
Coolidge administrations (thus helping to justify their tax cuts), it
was actually the earlier investment that had left American industry
poised for a boom.

One sector after another adopted the recipe of high wages, low
prices, and standardized production that Henry Ford had pioneered

in making his cars. Indeed, automobiles led the way to the new prosperity. The mass production of cars in the 1910s led to mass consumption in the 1920s, and the end of the war uncorked a buying frenzy. In 1919, fewer than 7 million automobiles dotted the nation's roads; by 1929, there were 23 million. Automobility, moreover, not only represented a huge part of the economy, it enabled other businesses to thrive as well.

Other numbers told similar tales of growth. Electricity, limited to just 16 percent of households in 1912, had reached more than 60 percent by the mid-1920s. Its spread launched new industries, too. The radio—a fad in 1922, with sales of only $60 million—became a household necessity by the decade's end; annual sales climbed to $842 million. A hot housing market created millions of new home owners; the greatest property boom of the decade, on the coasts of south Florida, made many Americans instantly rich—at least those who cashed in before the bubble burst in 1925 and 1926. (Even William Jennings Bryan moved to Florida and secured a small fortune with a series of well-timed investments and promotional activities. "Miami," quipped Bryan, "is the only city in the world where you can tell a lie at breakfast that will come true by evening.") A romance with credit—installment buying, layaway plans—stimulated consumption, while an army of clever young advertising men refined the craft of piquing new consumer desires instead of just sating existing ones. The result was an expanding middle class with more leisure time, more disposable income, and a greater appetite than ever before for fashionable clothing, iceboxes, sewing machines, phonographs, movie tickets, and more. "For nearly seven years," Frederick Lewis Allen recorded—a septennium that neatly encompassed Coolidge's presidency—"the prosperity bandwagon rolled down Main Street."[3]

How much any president should receive credit or blame for the course of the economy on his watch is impossible to determine. For Coolidge, the question is especially tricky. After the crash of 1929 and the Great Depression, the brand of economics to which he subscribed would be widely discredited, faulted for the disasters that followed. In retrospect, its many errors are evident. But to most people living in the 1920s—with some important exceptions—such policies appeared responsible for the glorious bounty. In any case, Coolidge Prosperity became the central issue in determining how people viewed the president and experienced the mood of public life under his leadership.

• • •

Coolidge's views on political economy originated in the values he learned in rural Vermont. Disinclined to reflection or ideological dogmatism, Coolidge simply translated his boyhood lessons into a quest for low taxes, low spending, balanced budgets, and light regulation. "His demand for economy," said Bascom Slemp, was "based on the stern judgment of the moralist as well as the sound reasoning of the economist."[4]

Coolidge's deputy in implementing these policies was Andrew Mellon, touted by conservatives as the greatest Treasury secretary since Alexander Hamilton. Sixty-eight years old, Mellon was a Pittsburgh banker and industrialist—Alcoa, the aluminum monopoly, was first among his many holdings—and the third-richest man in America, behind John D. Rockefeller and Henry Ford. Having survived the age of the robber barons without suffering its ravages, Mellon entered the 1920s with his faith in the capitalist gospel undimmed. His 1924 book, *Taxation: The People's Business*, presented a plan for fiscal reform that would eliminate the prevailing wartime tax system, which he blamed for "lawful evasion" of tax payments and the "withdrawal of capital from productive business."[5]

With his fastidious grooming and air of refinement, Mellon scarcely resembled Coolidge in manner or background. But on economics the two men saw eye to eye. Under Coolidge, Mellon continued, as he had under Harding, to champion the goals of cutting spending, taxes, and regulations. More than anything else, it was Mellon's role that made liberal critics such as Walter Lippmann see the Harding and Coolidge years as a restoration of the Gilded Age plutocracy. Mellon's name would be affixed to the various tax cuts that both presidents signed into law, and in time Coolidge became so reliant on his Treasury secretary that he installed a direct line between their offices—even though, partial to old habits, he normally disdained the telephone as a newfangled gadget unbefitting a president. Mellon, who had never much admired Harding, reciprocated the new president's esteem.

In shaping the nation's fiscal policy, Mellon and Coolidge benefited from the 1921 Budget and Accounting Act. A product of the Progressive Era's enthusiasm for efficient, rationalized administration, the act created the Bureau of the Budget, which made it a presidential duty to set forth an annual schedule of income and outgo. (Previously the various executive departments had prepared their own budgets for Congress to reconcile.) Harding's first budget director, Charles Dawes, zealously advocated for economy in government, setting a tone of budget-mindedness for the entire period.

The core of the Mellon tax plan was what critics would soon call "trickle down" economics: the idea that cutting taxes on the rich (or providing them with subsidies) would lead them to invest their windfall and spur productive advances that would benefit workers and consumers alike. Coolidge made the case in terms that Ronald Reagan would later echo. "If we had a tax whereby on the first working day the government took 5 percent of your wages, on the second day 10 percent," and so on throughout the week, he asked a Republican audience in February 1924, amid his first legislative fight for tax cuts, "how many of you would continue to work on the last two days of the week?" By removing disincentives to work, the government would encourage business to invest.[6]

In 1921, under Harding, Mellon had passed his first set of tax cuts. The main target was not the basic income tax rate, which had remained low throughout the 1920s—when Coolidge took office the brackets were set at 4 and 8 percent of a taxpayer's income—but the so-called surtaxes that had been imposed during World War I on citizens with incomes of more than $6,000 ($68,000 in 2006 dollars). Factoring in these surtaxes, the topmost tax bracket effectively reached 70 percent. Mellon's 1921 bill lowered this top rate to 50 percent—he wanted it even lower—and during Coolidge's tenure he would push through three more reductions. At the same time, he allowed corporate taxes to rise slightly—they inched up from 10 percent to 13½ percent, then back down to 12 percent— but that small increase was more than offset by the outright abolition of other wartime levies on business.[7]

Trickle-down economics enjoyed popular support for several reasons. First, the Coolidge-Mellon plan included not just rate cuts for the rich but other discounts that benefited the middle class, such as an across-the-board income tax cut in 1924 and an increased exemption for married couples in 1926. As a result, by the end of Coolidge's second term most Americans paid no federal income taxes at all. "Exemptions have been increased," Coolidge boasted in December 1927, "until 115 million people make out but 2.5 million individual taxable returns." State and local taxes, to be sure, were rising: during the 1920s many states imposed their first sales and gasoline taxes, and by mid-decade local property taxes consumed more than a quarter of the average farmer's income. Nonetheless, most Americans—with their federal tax bills eliminated and their standards of living rising—had no reason to protest Mellon's cuts. And while the bounty that the rich enjoyed sapped the U.S. Treasury of funds it might have used for other ends, the rising productivity masked the dangers of this public investment deficit. Mellon, in fact, continued to claim that broadening the tax burden across society was a positive good.[8]

Prosperity also restored to business a cachet it had lost in the Progressive Era. "The dollar is our Almighty," wrote the journalist Silas Bent. "Prosperity is considered a kind of morality, and no one has preached the doctrine more devoutly than Messrs. Coolidge, Hoover, and Mellon." It became common to justify in spiritual terms the materialist consumer culture that was supplanting the older ethic of hard work and pride in one's craft. Clergymen and Rotary Club members spoke of profit making as the Lord's work. Bruce Barton crystallized the alliance in his 1925 book *The Man Nobody Knows*. A bestseller, the book depicted Jesus as "the founder of modern business," his parables as "the most powerful advertisements of all time," the apostles as "twelve men from the bottom ranks of business . . . forged . . . into an organization that conquered the world." As Mencken noted, "The successful businessman . . . enjoys the public respect and adulation that elsewhere bathe only bishops and generals."[9]

A regard for business interests also shaped Coolidge's tariff policies. Where pure laissez-faire doctrine would have dictated an opposition to trade barriers, Coolidge believed government had a positive duty to promote productivity. Under Harding, the Fordney-McCumber Tariff Act had raised duties on imports, to the satisfaction of many American manufacturers, and Coolidge kept the rates high. Fordney-McCumber let the president raise or lower individual tariffs, and when Coolidge used this power he almost always raised them. Coolidge also inherited (and declined to change) a Tariff Commission populated with representatives of the industries it controlled—an unholy arrangement that lasted until eventually Congress cried foul.

On regulatory policy, too, Coolidge generally aligned himself with large corporations—here, typically, by keeping government intrusion to a minimum. Again, the tenor was set by the relative laxity with which Coolidge's appointees enforced the laws. At the Federal Trade Commission, Coolidge installed William Humphrey, who called his own agency "an instrument of oppression and disturbance and injury" to industry and curtailed its monitoring of unfair practices. The Food and Drug Administration was denied inspectors. The Interstate Commerce Commission, once an essential counterweight to the railroads, lapsed into fecklessness. Later in his term, Coolidge would allow radio, among other new industries, to emerge under regulatory regimes beneficial to a few leading firms—creating a near-monopoly that the networks would enjoy for decades. And although Coolidge's administration brought a record seventy antitrust suits, it settled almost a third of them on terms favorable to the company under scrutiny. (National Cash Register, for example, was convicted of price fixing, but its fine was lowered from $2,000 to $50.) The urgency with which the progressive presidents had put government to work supervising or curtailing corporate power was dissipating fast.[10]

Finally, Coolidge mostly opposed new federal programs. With large corporations starting to offer some benefits to their workers under the philosophy of "welfare capitalism," the demand for government to provide such aid was far from universal, and Coolidge considered such demands narrow and self-serving. He vigorously fought the effort to grant bonuses to World War I veterans and twice vetoed the McNary-Haugen bill, a deeply flawed scheme intended to help ailing farmers. He tried to minimize federal expenditures in response to the catastrophic 1927 Mississippi flood. And he acquiesced in a brief extension of the 1922 Sheppard-Towner Maternity and Infancy Act that gave funds to the states to create prenatal and child health care programs, on the condition that it begin "the gradual withdrawal of the federal government from this field." "The president recommended it in one paragraph of his budget message," one of its advocates complained, "and took it back in the next."[11]

Coolidge's commitment to a hands-off government should not be overdrawn. Like other officials who have favored pruning costs, he could shelve his principles when politics or mere gut preference inclined him to back a program—or, in the day-to-day way that people approach problems, he could simply fail to realize that grand principles ought to apply in a given case. In any event, forces more profound than a liberal fondness for the emerging welfare state or the desire of legislators to please constituents with pork-barrel spending were exerting pressure on the federal budget. Even as the fires of progressivism cooled, the public retained an appetite for social benefits and relief, and Coolidge was in no position to reverse these expectations. He acquiesced, for instance, by starting the construction of federal buildings in downtown Washington to house federal agencies, after Mellon convinced him it would be cheaper than renting the space in perpetuity. He doled out matching grants to states and cities for building roads—a far cry from the massive initiatives Dwight Eisenhower would authorize in the 1950s but still an admission of the need for some federal role in such projects. After the failure of the arms control talks he pursued, he green-lighted fifteen new cruisers for the navy, and he supported spending on the Boulder Dam in Colorado. But these policies represented the exceptions of his presidency, not the rule.

Economists and citizens alike still debate the merits of the economic philosophy that underpinned Coolidge's policies—the modified laissez-faire system that allowed for government support of businesses that appeared to serve the general good. Until their recent revival, these ideas had stood discredited for decades; in the middle of the twentieth century, even many Republican leaders accepted the inevitability of a mixed economy. In the 1920s, however, before the spread of John Maynard Keynes's revolutionary economics— with its stress on income distribution, full employment, and stimulative spending—the alliance of government and business that Coolidge and Mellon supported enjoyed widespread legitimacy. Some observers even contrasted Coolidge's approach with an older, rawer laissez-faire and deemed it modern and enlightened.

. . .

Coolidge planned to introduce his economic agenda in his first State of the Union message of December 6, 1923. Newspaper editorials brimmed with anticipation. "It will be a short document," the *New York Times* disclosed, after hearing from the mysterious "White House spokesman." "There are indications also that there would be considerable 'snap' to it." As always, skeptics grumbled. "This country has been sitting around now holding its breath for weeks waiting for the wonderful message that is to emanate from the presidential brain," wrote Harold Ickes. "But having read, with splitting sides, *Have Faith in Massachusetts* back in 1920, I am not particularly interested in anything that may come from the Coolidge pen . . . message or no message." Still, because Coolidge had ostentatiously subordinated his own goals to Harding's unfinished agenda back in August, the December 6 speech would mark

the unveiling of his own plans, and the president's upcoming statement assumed the proportions of an inaugural—a presidential
debut.[12]

Much speculation focused on whether Coolidge would deliver
a written or oral message to Congress. Though presidents had traditionally done the former, Coolidge opted to follow Woodrow
Wilson's example and appear in person; breaking new ground,
moreover, he had the speech broadcast over the radio, the better to
reach the public directly. Bascom Slemp assembled a network of
stations that reached as far as Dallas and Kansas City to carry the
speech. The effort was a success: when the speech aired, listeners in
St. Louis marveled that they could hear the president turning his
pages.

Appearing before Congress at 12:30 on a Thursday afternoon,
Coolidge delivered a speech that was exceptional for its unexcep-
tionality. He proposed no sweeping program, no Wilsonian crusade,
only a farrago of proposals of a moderate nature, served up in a
commonsensical tone that captured the public mood. "Our main
problems are domestic problems," the president declared. He urged
Congress to make enacting the Mellon plan—reducing income tax
rates across the board, chopping the surtaxes on the very rich, and
abolishing wartime excise taxes—its "paramount" goal. From there,
he moved into a laundry list of the sort that had become standard
fodder for State of the Union messages. His litany included tighter
immigration policies, an antilynching law, stricter enforcement of
Prohibition, a constitutional amendment limiting child labor, and
the regulation of new industries such as radio and aviation. He
called for free medical assistance to disabled veterans but stood by
his insistence that Congress not grant World War I veterans their
much-demanded bonus.[13]

All but unanimously, newspapers (whose editorial boards were
heavily Republican) endorsed the speech. "Among the most remark-
able contributions to the philosophy of statecraft," read a typical
endorsement from the *Los Angeles Express*. Slemp, tasked with monitoring the public reaction, was delighted that praise overwhelmed

any criticism. Coolidge noted proudly that the acclaim for his State of the Union outstripped that for any of his previous addresses. Most important, he had succeeded in identifying himself with the issues of cutting taxes and spending, on which his stands enjoyed majority support. Buoyed by the response, Coolidge took the occasion two days later of the Gridiron Dinner—an annual Washington ritual at which politicians joined in feting the press corps—to confirm his intent to run for president in 1924.[14]

• • •

If Coolidge entered 1924 flying high with the public, on Capitol Hill he found himself stymied at almost every turn. Much of the fault was the president's own. Having spent his vice-presidential years mostly giving speeches, he was a novice at legislative relations. "No Republican President within memory had seemed to have so little contact with Congress and the rank and file," noted Samuel Ratcliffe, a well-known London journalist and student of American politics. Coolidge tried to court congressional leaders, summoning them to the White House after reading about developments on the Hill in the morning paper, and he also hosted them at White House breakfasts. But his diffidence at those sessions often left the lawmakers more confused than engaged.[15]

The bottom line was that much of Congress was unfriendly to his goals. Nominal Republican majorities concealed losses to the Democrats in the 1922 midterm elections and a serious internal GOP rift between the pro-business Old Guard and the unpredictable Progressives; the latter bloc often allied with Democrats, whether to dredge up the muck of Teapot Dome or thwart the president's legislative goals. Coolidge squared off against this bipartisan coalition in early 1924 on two pressing issues—taxes and the veterans' bonus—that became inextricably linked in a larger battle of the budget.

In 1924, the federal budget remained almost $2 billion smaller than its historic peak size of $5.1 billion (in 1921). Tax receipts were poised to generate a budget surplus. Although this surplus actually undermined Mellon's claim that wartime tax rates were stifling investment and depressing federal revenue—and thus the justification for his trickle-down cuts—public debate nonetheless revolved around how to spend the projected windfall. Most legislators wanted to reward World War I veterans with a bonus, arguing that the poor wages soldiers had earned, especially in contrast to the wartime prosperity others had enjoyed, had become a national embarrassment. But the measure on the table would cost the government an estimated $135 million in the first year and up to $2 billion over the long haul. Moreover, in the 1920s veterans were seen as a bloc that was both vaguely radical and narrowly self-interested, and in the days before Social Security and similar benefits their demand for the bonus struck many Americans as socialistic. For these reasons, Harding, reflecting the dominant Republican position, vetoed a bonus bill in 1922. When the American Legion renewed its agitation for the benefit in the fall of 1923, Coolidge resolved to do as his predecessor had.

Coolidge's budget for 1924, the smallest since before the war, pared spending in almost every government department. (The Labor Department, incurring greater expenses for immigration control, and Justice, with increases for penitentiaries, were exceptions.) Coolidge adamantly opposed the bonus, preferring to retire some of the federal debt while continuing Mellon's long-range program of lowering the income surtaxes. "If this business is showing a surplus of receipts," he said, referring to the government, "the taxpayer should share therein." To be sure, Harding and Mellon had already sliced the top tax rate to 50 percent in 1921, but the Treasury secretary now wanted to lower it to 25 percent. Such a reduction would cost hundreds of millions, and to pass both the bonus and the tax cuts was, for the budget-minded Coolidge, unthinkable.[16]

Coolidge expected to prevail. The president insisted that the bonus—along with the Bursum Bill, another measure gathering force in Congress, which would increase pensions for veterans of previous wars—would bust the budget. Repeating a line popular with bonus foes, Coolidge argued that such provisions would aid just a part of the populace, whereas his tax cuts would help the nation as a whole. But Congress had other ideas. In the late winter, sentiment for both the bonus and the Bursum Bill snowballed. Henry Cabot Lodge, increasingly rivalrous with the president, endorsed both measures. Republican Senate whip Charles Curtis, normally a loyal party man, introduced them on the Senate floor. Both passed, forcing a showdown with the president.

On May 3 Coolidge vetoed the Bursum Bill, declaring, "The advantage of a class cannot be greater than the welfare of a nation." He managed to sustain the veto in Congress. But when he vetoed the far more expensive bonus bill twelve days later—pronouncing archly that "patriotism . . . bought and paid for is not patriotism"— Congress mutinied. Within days, both chambers overrode the second veto, to open rejoicing in the packed galleries, "the likes of which," the New York Times reported, "has seldom been heard in the Senate."[17]

Meanwhile, the president's tax plan was faltering. Although across-the-board cuts on the meager basic rates spawned little protest, the plan to slash the all-important revenue-raising surtaxes was dead on arrival on the Hill. Despite Coolidge's claims that he was "inflexibly opposed" to any compromise, by mid-February, the New York Times reported, the goal of a 25 percent top rate was "hopelessly lost." Instead, Congress was debating whether to go down to 44 percent (as the Democrats preferred) or 35 percent (as most Republicans wished).[18]

At the same time, Republican senator James Couzens of Michigan, who was feuding with Mellon, demanded an investigation of the Bureau of Internal Revenue for having given special and costly tax rebates to large corporations. Couzens's investigations eventually showed that Mellon had delivered, almost for the asking, dubious handouts to several large companies, including some in which he himself had an interest. Totaling some $3.5 billion over the course of Mellon's tenure, these rebates were further augmented by the return of more than $80 million in inheritance taxes to the heirs of some of the nation's largest estates. Although it would take time before all Couzens's charges were borne out, and for all their sordidness they never managed to taint Coolidge's reputation for integrity, they nonetheless kept the administration on the defensive throughout the tax bill fight and ensured that the Mellon plan wouldn't pass Congress undiluted.

After much haggling—between Republicans and Democrats, the Senate and the House, the legislature and the executive—a deal was finally struck. The final bill cut the top surtax rate to 40 percent, raised the threshold for the surtax, accepted Mellon's rate reductions on the basic brackets, and—to Mellon's and Coolidge's dismay—imposed new levies on gifts and inheritances. The president made a show of agonizing over whether to sign the bill, retreating to the presidential yacht to ruminate rather than taking Congress's revisions lying down. But in the end he declared that for all its flaws the bill improved upon the existing tax code. On June 2, he signed it. Depicted in the press as another congressional rebuff to the president, in the longer arc of history the outcome represented another victory for Calvin Coolidge and his trickle-down creed.[19]

6

Controversies

In the 1920s Americans warred over a series of issues in which basic values were at stake, from Prohibition and immigration to the teaching of evolution and tolerance of the Ku Klux Klan. Indirectly, these fights occurred because liberalism was on the rise. For the first time city dwellers outnumbered rural residents, and secular cosmopolitan beliefs were spreading outward. Newly assertive African-Americans, many self-consciously calling themselves "New Negroes," established a vibrant presence in national life, demanding their overdue rights. The "New Woman" similarly challenged long-held gender boundaries in her dress, social, and sexual habits, and in her self-conception, even as the political intensity that had marked the suffrage movement subsided. The young in general flouted dominant mores on matters of personal freedom such as birth control and drinking—even as they too supported Coolidge and, tacitly, his management of the nation's economy.

Partly in response to this revolution in manners and morals, guardians of the old order mobilized politically in the 1920s. Some of these reactionary movements had reared their head in previous years with the revival of the Ku Klux Klan in 1915, Prohibition's passage in 1919, and the Red Scare of 1919–20. But in the 1920s, these forms of political fundamentalism gained strength.[1]

Sympathetic to neither the liberals nor the reactionaries and clinging to his belief in minimal presidential governance, Coolidge tried to avoid the culture wars. When he weighed in, he tried to minimize any backlash. He criticized, in passing, the prosecution of John Scopes for teaching evolution in a Tennessee high school class, but he kept his comments brief, making it clear that he didn't want the issue to provoke "even greater differences than the Prohibition amendment." He pardoned the remaining prisoners who sat convicted of sedition during the mad rush to punish dissenters during the war. He nominally supported Prohibition and served no liquor in the White House, but he tolerated a level of enforcement lax enough to leave most Americans, at least in "wet" states, free to drink. Although Coolidge's restraint in these areas had the virtue of keeping social strife from worsening, it also deprived him of the chance to cast himself squarely on the side of social progress.[2]

The first of the social issues to confront Coolidge was immigration. Since the 1880s, eastern and southern Europeans, including Catholics and a record number of Jews, had been flooding into American cities. Many Americans of northern European and Protestant descent, who had come to view "American" as synonymous with their own ethnic heritage, watched the changing complexion of the populace with alarm. In the late nineteenth century a nativist movement had arisen, and in 1917 Congress imposed, over Woodrow Wilson's veto, a literacy test on foreign settlers.

After the war, several factors heightened the nativists' distress. Labor radicalism fueled anxiety about the menace allegedly posed by the foreign-born, and the fight over the League of Nations laid bare ethnic divisions in the United States, exposing hostility toward foreigners as well. When in 1921 Ellis Island proved unable to handle the new boatloads of arriving Europeans—authorities diverted ships to Boston—Congress temporarily capped the number of immigrants who could enter the country.

By 1924, support was gathering across the political spectrum for stronger federal action. Voices of dissent were passionate but relatively few in number, coming mainly from immigrants, minorities, and city dwellers like New York City congressman Fiorello La Guardia. Never one to occupy the fringes of political opinion,

Coolidge endorsed new immigration caps in his 1923 State of the Union message, declaring, "America must be kept American." (Three years earlier, Coolidge had stated crudely that the Nordic race would decline if its people combined with those of other races—but on the whole his racial attitudes were neither especially enlightened nor especially benighted for his age.)[3]

Congress, however, needed no prodding from Coolidge to act. In the House, Republican Albert Johnson of Washington, a staunch nativist, led the charge. His bill proposed to limit each country's immigrants according to a formula based on the 1890 census, which meant severely curtailing the numbers of Jews, Italians, Greeks, and Slavs. Another provision barred the Japanese from immigrating altogether (as an 1882 law had barred most Chinese). Despite some fervent resistance—at one point two congressmen all but came to blows on the House floor—a lightly modified version of Johnson's bill passed the lower chamber. Moving less rashly, the Senate stalled in the face of the bill's barely disguised racism. Yet the Senate sponsor, Republican David Reed of Pennsylvania, essentially shared Johnson's goal of maintaining the ethnic status quo, and the general discriminatory thrust of preferring northwestern Europeans remained in the final version.

Though it would affect comparatively fewer immigrants, it was the Japanese-exclusion provision that proved the biggest sticking point, since Coolidge and his administration opposed the measure. Leading the fight was Secretary of State Charles Evans Hughes, a political heavyweight who had been governor of New York, an associate justice of the Supreme Court, and the Republican nominee for president in 1916. A middle-of-the-road internationalist, Hughes bristled at the isolationism he saw pervading Congress and argued against the Japanese-exclusion clause, insisting it would violate a 1907 "Gentleman's Agreement" between the United States and Japan. Under that pact, Japan had promised to limit emigration to the United States in return for guarantees that Japanese students already here would be integrated into the California schools. (Most Japanese-Americans lived in California.) If the immigration bill passed, Hughes warned, it would fly in the face of that delicately negotiated entente and harm relations with Japan. With Coolidge's backing, he pressed the Senate to make room for a quota of Japanese.

Unfortunately, Hughes hurt his cause with a tactical blunder. Having been cautioned by the Japanese ambassador, Masanao Hanihara, of "grave consequences" should the ban become law, Hughes relayed the ambassador's warning to the Senate. A huge flap resulted. Lawmakers took umbrage at what Senator Hiram Johnson of California called an "impertinent" threat and an infringement on American "sovereignty." An anti-Japanese backlash followed, and the Senate upheld the exclusion with scant dissent.[4]

The reconciliation of the House and Senate drafts offered one last chance to obtain a more moderate bill. But Coolidge was ineffectual, and a meager amendment that he had gotten inserted in the Senate bill was dropped altogether. Coolidge let his unhappiness with the Japanese exclusion be known and, as with the tax bill, made noises about vetoing the immigration bill. But he never considered that option seriously.

In fact, the dustup over the Japanese exclusion obscured the broad support enjoyed by the bill's core provisions. Once the bill gathered steam, its limits on southern and eastern European immigration never came under serious challenge. Coolidge personally rebuffed a group led by Rabbi Stephen Wise and New York congressman Samuel Dickstein who sought to plead their case against the new quotas. Eventually Coolidge capitulated altogether. Sensing defeat, he signed the bill, Japanese exclusion and all, on May 26. As a result, only a tiny number of immigrants would enter the United States over the next four decades, profoundly affecting the demographic and political character of the nation. After the Holocaust of the 1930s and '40s, the bill would come to be seen as a betrayal of the nation's promise of an open door—one that, along with its other unfortunate effects, helped consign millions of European Jews to death. Not until a major new immigration law was passed in 1965 would America's doors open again.

• • •

Although restricting immigration enjoyed widespread support, its most enthusiastic backers included the members of the resurgent Ku Klux Klan. In the 1920s the Klan itself became another hot-button issue. Again, Coolidge would try to avoid the fray.

Originally founded after the Civil War by Confederate veterans, the white-robed, hooded vigilante group had died out after vigorous prosecution by the Grant administration in the 1870s. But in 1915, a Methodist preacher in Stone Mountain, Georgia, reconstituted the infamous brotherhood. Preaching not only white supremacy but also the inferiority of Catholics and Jews, he won few adherents until the early 1920s, when membership mushroomed to five million— not only in the South but also in other rural regions where old-stock Protestants feared the swelling urban masses. States as diverse as Colorado, Indiana, Kansas, Maine, Ohio, and Oregon all claimed influential Klan populations, and numerous senators, governors, and state legislators around the country owed their election to the body's support. While most of the Klan's middle-class members eschewed violence, viewing the association as little different from a Rotary Club, others carried out lynchings, beatings, brandings, and arson, frequently gaining acquittals from juries of their white peers.

In 1925 the "Grand Dragon" of the Klan's Indiana chapter, David Stephenson, would go to prison for complicity in the death of a woman he had raped, hastening the organization's demise. But during the 1924 election season the Klan remained a contentious subject. At the Democratic National Convention in July, no issue divided the party more deeply. Delegates battled over whether to repudiate the group and risk alienating key supporters, especially in the South. Their refusal to do so, except obliquely, demoralized the party's liberal members and created a public relations fiasco, since public opinion on the whole reviled the Klan.

Coolidge and the Republicans showed ample hesitation of their own. In the 1920s, most black voters were Republicans, while the Democrats still commanded solid support across the South. But the GOP's conservative stands on issues like immigration and alcohol recommended it to Klansmen in states such as Colorado and New Jersey, and many Republicans feared the costs of denouncing the Klan outright. When, despite his party's equivocations, the Democratic presidential nominee, John W. Davis, finally did speak out against the vigilante group in the summer of 1924, he shrewdly called on the president to do likewise. Black leaders, Jewish leaders, and the New York Republican Party, among others, all joined in the pressure on Coolidge to do so.

But the president spoke only in generalities. The few statements about the Klan emanating from any White House spokesman were elliptical and somewhat cryptic reassurances from Bascom Slemp that Coolidge was "not a member of the order and is not in sympathy with the aims and purposes." That Coolidge gave the job of delivering this anodyne message to Slemp—a racist southerner whose appointment as the president's secretary the NAACP had earlier called "a slap in the face" to twelve million black Americans—only made it more suspect. To be sure, Coolidge had no affection for the Klan; his silence was strategic, and it may have helped him win the electoral votes of Colorado, Indiana, and Kansas. But Coolidge's lack of comment couldn't be written off solely as election-year caution. In August 1925 the president again refused a chance to speak out. With 40,000 robed Klan members descending on Washington and marching past the White House, the president made good on his Silent Cal moniker by vacationing in Swampscott, Massachusetts, and issuing no denunciation. Later, in October 1925, he gave a high-minded address to the American Legion in Omaha, praising men of all races and religions as equally American and having fought with equal valor in the army. But he did not mention the Klan by name.[5]

Like most Americans, Coolidge considered himself an egalitarian, and his record on racial issues compares favorably to that of Woodrow Wilson and many other contemporaries. But the mildness of his opposition to the Klan typified his lack of leadership on racial issues. Though the 1920s witnessed the Harlem Renaissance, Marcus Garvey's black nationalist movement, social science research that decimated pseudoscientific racist claims, and activism by the NAACP and the Urban League, the will to reform in Washington— including in the White House—was still lacking. In his 1923 State of the Union address, Coolidge deemed racial difficulties "to a large extent local problems which must be worked out by the mutual forbearance and human kindness of each community" rather than by "outside interference." While calling for antilynching legislation, he lent the bill emerging from the House only tepid support when it stood a fair chance of congressional passage in 1925, spending his political capital instead on another round of tax cuts. The bill died.[6]

On other racial matters, Coolidge's record was marked by half-hearted efforts and qualifications. In 1924, he supported replacing black Republican delegates from southern states with white ones in order to attract more voters there. He never made a priority of enforcing black voting rights, and his efforts to reverse Wilson's policy of segregating the federal workforce were halting and partial. If he deserves credit for commuting the jail sentence of Marcus Garvey, who was imprisoned for mail fraud—Attorney General John Sargent, reviewing the case, could find no one claiming to have been defrauded—Coolidge had the freed activist deported to his native Jamaica. Other actions—proposing a biracial commission to foster "mutual understanding," which came to naught, and the appointment of a few blacks to government posts, such as ambassador to Liberia—smacked of tokenism.

Even Coolidge's superficially liberal attitudes and fine words on race masked blind spots. As Bruce Barton reported in 1923, Coolidge lectured a black audience that while he admired "their progress," they should recall that "the Anglo-Saxon race has been centuries in reaching its present position and that the Negro could not and must not expect to bridge the chasm in a century." Civil rights leaders lamented what they saw as lip service to their cause. The civil rights leader A. Philip Randolph recalled joining William Monroe Trotter, editor of the *Boston Guardian* and a Massachusetts acquaintance of Coolidge's, on a visit to see the president. After Trotter "made a very fiery talk," Randolph recalled, Coolidge said simply, "All right, thank you very much," and sat down. Then, said Randolph, "Trotter turns right around with his group and we walked out." The behavior, typical of Coolidge, was no less disappointing because other visitors received similar treatment. And while the president's indifference didn't stop most politically active blacks from backing him in 1924, any hopes that the Party of Lincoln would deliver more justice than Wilson's Democrats were already dashed. "May God write us down as asses if ever again we are found putting our trust in either the Republican or Democratic parties," said the great civil rights leader W. E. B. DuBois.[7]

• • •

Classically conservative on economic policy and averse to progressive leadership on social policy, Coolidge was in foreign affairs a cautious moderate: cognizant that America needed to play a leading role in world affairs yet wary of grand Wilsonian projects and eager not to run afoul of public sentiment. Neither isolationist nor imperialist, he hoped to encourage peace and stability without becoming unduly entangled in Europe's affairs.

On the international front, Coolidge had to confront several important issues in his first year in office, including the question of whether to establish diplomatic relations with the Soviet Union and calls for various treaties and institutions to protect the peace. But the most urgent and knottiest issues were those surrounding foreign debt to the United States. During World War I, American banks had lent the European allies more than $10 billion, and after the war these nations, their economies ailing, were struggling to meet their payments. Then crisis struck. In early 1923, Germany, groaning under the reparations imposed by the Versailles Treaty, defaulted on its payments to France. French and Belgian troops moved into the Ruhr Valley, home to the German coal and steel industries, raising the prospect of another war. Germany printed money to pay its debts, resulting in a legendary period of hyperinflation. By October 1923, one dollar bought 4.2 trillion marks.

Inheriting this crisis, Coolidge hewed to his old-fashioned notions of fiscal responsibility. Some experts were proposing that Europe's debts be wiped clean in the interest of economic stability, with the forgiveness tallied as an American gift to the war effort. But Coolidge, like Harding before him, resisted. Along with much of the American public, he believed that debts should be repaid, plain and simple. "Well, they hired the money, didn't they?" he is alleged to have said. Nor did he deign to consider lowering the high tariffs on imports that he and Harding both supported—a move that would have helped the European economies by encouraging exports to the United States.[8]

The Franco-German crisis forced Coolidge to take action, however, and Secretary of State Hughes secured the president's blessing to organize a commission of delegates from Belgium, France, Britain, Italy, and the United States to craft a solution. To lead it, Coolidge named the dynamic Charles Dawes, a wealthy financier who had been Harding's economy-minded budget director. Though the president stayed out of the negotiations, he threw his weight behind the Dawes Committee and joined its fortunes to his own. Negotiations commenced in earnest in Paris in January 1924, and by early April a compromise emerged: in return for a withdrawal from the Ruhr, the Allies would restructure the German debt and reorganize the German central bank. Providing the critical ingredient, the United States would furnish Germany with the capital to help repay its loans. Despite criticism from isolationists like Hiram Johnson, who decried the meddling in European affairs, Coolidge stuck with the plan.

Overall, Americans were relieved to see continental tensions defused. Although Germany balked at the terms, it signed the agreement in late August, to much celebration. The Dawes Plan helped the European economies in the short term, spurring a boom in Germany that lasted through much of the 1920s. They also paved the way for the 1925 Locarno agreements, which resolved some outstanding territorial disputes and promised to establish a spirit of cooperation among the European powers, winning praise from Coolidge as likely to have "a great and permanent effect upon

humanity." In 1925, Dawes shared the Nobel Peace Prize with
Austen Chamberlain, the British statesman who had spearheaded
the Locarno talks.[9]

Alas, the German boom and the "spirit of Locarno" would prove
short-lived—especially after the 1929 Wall Street crash put an end
to America's ability to prop up the European economies. In retrospect, there was something absurd all along about the shell game—
American funds going to Germany, through the Allies, and back to
the United States—which was contrived partly to satisfy each country's sense of amour propre. Still, when the Dawes Plan was signed,
few people foresaw dire consequences. In the summer of 1924 the
resolution of the European crisis, however temporary, enhanced
Coolidge's popularity. Without making official pledges on behalf of
the government, he had, through the work of a private citizen, gotten private banks to solve a crisis. The move reassured Americans
that peace was at hand.

As it turned out, Coolidge's troubles with Congress in 1924
didn't hurt him much either. His legislative losses may actually
have helped him as much as his victories. They spared him any
wrath from veterans and any possible fallout from skewed tax cuts,
while he received credit for what the newspapers presented (in the
mocking words of newspaperman Frank Kent) as "the forceful and
vigorous talk of a red-blooded, resolute, two-fisted, fighting executive." He had spoken directly to the public and felt confident they
backed his leadership. "Coolidge personifies to our people calmness,
common sense, and splendid courage," Dawes later wrote. Buoyed
by the economy, emphasizing his modest aims and his rectitude,
and drawing attention to his own virtue, Coolidge pinned his success or failure on concerns greater than mere acts of legislation.
Like the best politicians, he made such judgment hinge on who
he was.[10]

The fall campaign was looming.

7

Getting Elected

Whatever setbacks Coolidge's antagonists in Congress dealt to his agenda, they did not slow his march toward the Republican presidential nomination in 1924. In fact, despite a meager record of achievement and no real base in his party, the president sewed up the prize with relative ease. When he assumed the presidency in August 1923, he had struck many as a placeholder, destined to ride out Harding's term until a worthy successor, such as his ambitious Commerce secretary, Herbert Hoover, could take over. At that time, vice presidents were not considered heirs apparent. Apart from the inimitable Theodore Roosevelt, no vice president who inherited the presidency had won so much as his own party's nomination in the next election cycle: not John Tyler in 1844 nor Millard Fillmore in 1852 nor Andrew Johnson in 1868 nor Chester Arthur in 1884.

Many observers in 1923 thought Coolidge had no greater claim to a full term than those hapless presidents of yesteryear. Certainly, he had yet to achieve what the political vernacular of a later day would call *gravitas*. With the Republican Party in "virtual chaos," wrote Richard Oulahan of the *New York Times*, exhibiting the misplaced certainty characteristic of many political pundits, "the national convention . . . will not be a ratification meeting."[1]

Some wiser heads realized that Coolidge planned to seek the office in his own right. He was, *Literary Digest* noted on August 23, "already an avowed and formidable candidate for the next Republican nomination." The president wasted no time in buttressing his position. Showing a political skill he didn't bring to his battles on the Hill, he methodically disposed of his major rivals for the nomination.[2]

First to go was Pennsylvania governor Gifford Pinchot—Theodore Roosevelt's old friend and ally, a leader of the Progressive Republicans, and a serious contender for the 1924 nomination. Just weeks after acceding to the presidency, Coolidge turned a potentially nettlesome labor dispute in the anthracite coal mines of Pennsylvania into an occasion to co-opt Pinchot—and, in the process, defuse an explosive situation.

In 1900 and 1902, and again in 1919, miners had struck for better wages and working conditions. In the 1920s, they were agitating anew, sowing fear about continued public access to a vital source of energy, as well as about the return of labor radicalism. But Coolidge glimpsed an opportunity. In 1902, Pinchot had urged Roosevelt to take the unprecedented step of setting up a commission to mediate the debilitating strike, which the president did to great acclaim. Now, in August 1923, with another strike looming, Pinchot offered the new president his services as a mediator, expecting to receive some glory as the election year approached. Coolidge responded by inviting Pinchot and John Hays Hammond, chairman of the U.S. Coal Commission, to lunch at the White House, where he accepted Pinchot's offer of help. The president stated publicly, however, that Pinchot would be following the administration's guidance in pursuing a deal, angering Pinchot but still binding him to his role.

Pinchot was left to carry out the hard work of negotiation, which he performed creditably. The miners walked off the job on September 1, but within a week Pinchot cobbled together a deal that gave them a 10 percent wage increase. As a result, the governor scored points with those sympathetic to the miners—but so did Coolidge, who also dispelled impressions lingering from 1919 that he was reflexively anti-labor. The Republican Party's conservatives, however, blamed Pinchot, and not the president, for appeasing the agitators.

Mellon, who owned a Pennsylvania coal-mining company, held enough sway with his state's delegation to make sure it didn't rally behind a Pinchot candidacy. In a few months' time, Pinchot, outplayed, threw his support to Coolidge.

A more troublesome rival was the automaker Henry Ford. Though Ford had lost a Senate bid from Michigan in 1918, running as a Democrat, he remained extremely popular as a businessman—in no small part for dramatically raising his workers' wages—but also as a public figure. In many quarters his plainspoken and populistic pronouncements passed for wisdom. Scenarios being bruited about envisioned the Republican Party drafting Ford for its nomination or his running as an independent. But the president co-opted Ford as well. In December, just as Coolidge was formally declaring his own presidential bid, he met with the automaker at the White House, where—not to put too fine a point on it—he seems to have bought him off.

The apparent deal with Ford centered on the dam and factories on the Tennessee River at Muscle Shoals, Alabama, where the Wilson administration had begun generating hydroelectric power and making fertilizer. Opposed in principle to state ownership of industry, Coolidge and other conservatives had long wanted to privatize the holdings. Soon after meeting with Ford, the president asked Congress to sell the carmaker the properties. Then, on December 19, Ford retrieved his hat from the ring, declaring, "I would never for a moment think of running against Calvin Coolidge for president." And although the Muscle Shoals deal never went through—an outraged Senator George Norris of Nebraska blocked it—the timing raised eyebrows. "Did Mr. Coolidge bribe Mr. Ford with a renewed offer of Muscle Shoals?" the *New York Times* asked bluntly. Or did Ford think "more of getting rid of his own surtaxes than . . . of righting the wrongs of the plain people?" Regardless, Republican officials exulted that Coolidge was now a shoo-in for the nomination.[3]

By the new year, Coolidge had largely clinched the nomination. Slemp delivered southern delegates to Coolidge's camp and shored up support among the Old Guard. Chief Justice Taft brought party power brokers in line. Progressive discontent remained, with hopes centering on Hiram Johnson and Robert La Follette. But while Johnson fanned the Teapot Dome investigations and fought Coolidge's agenda—he spearheaded the fights for Japanese exclusion and against the tax cuts and the Dawes Plan—and even won a primary election in South Dakota, he never posed a serious threat. La Follette, for his part, chose to run with Montana Democrat Burton Wheeler under the banner of a reconstituted Progressive Party. Although they attracted the support of midwestern farmers and struck many prominent politicians and intellectuals as the only tolerable ticket, the Progressives never had more than the faintest hopes of victory.

Contrary to Richard Oulahan's forecast, the Republican convention, which opened June 10 in a sleek new 15,000-seat skylighted arena in Cleveland, was a far cry from the nail-biting saga of 1920. Butler ran the show, helped by Stearns and Slemp. To reach the widest possible audience, they invited in the radio networks for the first time. To celebrate the president's economic policies, they trotted out Mellon, the embodiment of prosperity, to kick off the convention—which he did to deafening applause. Finally, to drive home the message of party unanimity, they made sure that no one was nominated besides the president. On the first ballot Coolidge gained 1,165 of the 1,209 votes. Johnson and La Follette, who had not yet bolted for a third party, each netted a handful from the rural upper Midwest, where Coolidge was weak because he opposed aggressive relief measures for farmers. It turned out to be a coronation after all.

What drama remained surrounded the vice-presidential choice. It eventually went to Dawes. Flush with publicity from his leadership on European debt, Dawes was charmingly blunt; he shocked sensibilities by peppering his speech with profanities like "hell," which were then raw to many ears. Though Coolidge and Butler had courted the Progressive senator William Borah of Idaho, who declined the offer, Dawes was more than acceptable. He had had a proud career in both private and public service, and his parsimony appealed to Coolidge. Not least, he was certain to revel in the fall stumping that was the running mate's main task.

Coolidge found even more cause for optimism when the Democrats convened in New York City on June 24. Deeply torn over the Klan and Prohibition, the party struggled to find a nominee. New York governor Alfred Smith, a Catholic who was anti-Klan and "wet," had the support of the cities and the East; Wilson's son-in-law and Treasury secretary, the Georgia-born William McAdoo, a "dry" who enjoyed Klan support, was popular in the West and South. But both men had fatal flaws. Smith's Catholicism was thought to be a liability, while McAdoo's bit part in Teapot Dome—he had taken a $25,000 payment from the corrupt businessman Edward Doheny—threatened to annul whatever advantage the scandal might afford the Democrats. Stalemate ensued.

Ten days and a record 102 ballots passed with no resolution. The nation again listened on radio, but this time fascination curdled into horror as the deadlock persisted, with ugly rhetoric abounding. The Democrats retained a censor to keep any offensive speech off the airwaves, but to spare themselves public revulsion, they would have had to censor the convention itself. Finally, on the 103rd ballot, they settled on John W. Davis, a West Virginia native, a former solicitor general and ambassador to Great Britain, and a corporate lawyer whose firm, Davis, Polk, held prestige with the white-shoe class but not the rank and file. Despite denouncing the Klan over the summer, he was sufficiently retrograde on racial politics to appeal to the party's white supremacists. (Davis would end his career in 1954 defending segregation before the Supreme Court in *Brown v. Board of Education*.) To run with Davis, the Democrats selected Nebraska governor Charles Bryan, the younger brother of their thrice-failed presidential nominee, William Jennings Bryan, creating the bizarre coupling of a Wall Street insider with a scourge of Wall Street.

As the Democrats immolated themselves in Madison Square Garden and the Progressives met quixotically in Cleveland to nominate La Follette, Coolidge—having accepted a tax bill he thought too mild, taken credit for an immigration bill he thought imperfect, and gloried in a popular European debt plan that would prove feckless—looked placidly at what were turning out to be bright prospects for his election.

. . .

Nonetheless, the summer of 1924 was not to be a time of celebration for the president. Closer to home, terrible misfortune was to deprive his election campaign—and, he later said, his entire presidency—of its glory.

On Monday, June 30, the president's two sons were playing tennis on the White House courts when sixteen-year-old Calvin Jr., wearing sneakers but no socks, developed a blood blister on the middle toe of his right foot. Two days later, the boy began to feel weak and tired. White House doctors examined him. A 102-degree fever, swollen glands, and red streaks on his leg suggested a bacterial infection. The next day, tests confirmed that a staphylococcus had poisoned his bloodstream.

Modern antibiotics for treating such infections were unknown at the time. Not for another four years would Alexander Fleming happen upon the curative powers of the penicillium fungus, and penicillin as a drug wouldn't come into use until the 1940s. In 1924, doctors could try only injections of the antidotes then in currency: mercurochrome, a mercury-based compound, and a staphylococcus-based antigen designed to stimulate the production of antibodies. Neither serum worked.[4]

During the week Calvin Jr. was increasingly confined to bed at the White House. As the severity of the illness dawned on the president, he became deeply distressed. When he dined with Dawes at the White House, the new vice-presidential nominee noted that Coolidge "seemed to lose all interest in the conversation, and the dinner soon ended." Coolidge wrote to his father that although Calvin Jr. was receiving "all that medical science can give him," his recovery was uncertain. "He may have a long illness with ulcers," Coolidge noted; "then again he may be better in a few days." But the boy's condition worsened.[5]

Powerless to help, the president poignantly tried to cheer up his son. Knowing the boy's love of furry animals, Coolidge waded into the shrubbery around the White House to capture a small brown rabbit, which he eagerly delivered to Calvin Jr. The boy flashed an appreciative smile, and the president, for the time being, returned to his work.[6]

As his son's condition deteriorated, however, the president found himself unable to think about anything else. "The president was a stricken man," Edmund Starling observed, "going about as if in a dream." On Friday, July 4, the Democrats were meeting in New York and the Progressives in Cleveland, but the president's birthday passed without celebration at the White House. The next day doctors took Calvin Jr. to the Walter Reed Army Hospital for surgery, giving the Coolidges some hope, and on Sunday the president wrote to his father in Vermont that the operation seemed to have been a success. Yet he was mistaken. The staphylococcus continued to spread through Calvin Jr.'s system, and soon he was alternating between sleep and delirium. The president and first lady waited by their son's side at Walter Reed.[7]

By July 7, a week after the injury, Calvin Jr. was slipping away. The president sat for much of that Monday simply gazing at his son. At one point the boy hallucinated that he was riding backward on a horse and called out to be turned around. The president reached over, held his son, and turned him, in the vain hope of giving the boy some satisfaction. Later, the president pressed into his son's hand his treasured gold locket containing a photo of Victoria Coolidge and a lock of her hair. But the boy, who was lapsing into a coma, kept dropping it. Repeatedly, the locket would fall to the floor and the president would pick it up and hand it to his son. "In his suffering he was asking me to make him well," the president recalled stoically. "I could not."[8]

By nightfall, Calvin Jr. was unaware of his surroundings. At 10:20 P.M., he died.

Calvin Jr. was the first child of a sitting president to die since 1862, when Abraham Lincoln's eleven-year-old son Willie succumbed to typhoid fever. The nation reacted with a commensurate outpouring of grief. Letters and telegrams flooded the White House. The Democrats—still bickering and dickering over their nominee in Madison Square Garden—adjourned immediately for the night, all traces of rancor evaporating from the hall. In Plymouth Notch, John Coolidge heard of his grandson's death by radio and walked over to the family plot where Victoria and Abigail lay buried.[9]

The president and Grace were devastated. Grace bore the loss more easily than her husband. Her comments about her late son contained warm memories of happy moments she had spent with him and a serene confidence that "in a very real sense he is with us." Coolidge, in contrast, felt deep despair for months. One night, when the boy's corpse was lying in state in the East Room, the president came into the room wearing his bathrobe after the callers had all left and stood staring sadly at the coffin, caressing his son's hair. For months his demeanor remained funereal. "His face," a friend noted, "had the bleak desolation of cold November rain beating on gray Vermont granite." The president often said that he was never the same again.[10]

Visitors attested to the emotional toll Coolidge bore. A reporter who paid a call on the president in his office remarked on the open and uncharacteristic flood of feeling: "His voice trembled and tears ran down his cheeks. He was not the president of the United States. He was the father, overcome by grief and by love for his boy. He wept unafraid, unashamed." To another White House caller, the president noted, "When I look out that window, I always see my boy playing tennis on that court out there." When Edmund Starling came upon a child outside the White House who asked to meet Coolidge "to tell him how sorry I am that his little boy died," the president, overcome with emotion, instructed his aide, "Whenever a boy wants to see me, always bring him in. Never turn one away or make him wait."[11]

Coolidge blamed himself for his son's death, following the tortuous chain of logic that if he hadn't been president, Calvin Jr. would never have injured himself on the White House grounds. He took solace in telling himself that "the ways of providence are often beyond our understanding," yet ultimately even Coolidge, with his appetite for pieties, couldn't accept this platitude as an explanation for the cruelty of the loss. "It seemed to me that the world had need of the work that it was probable he could do. I don't know why such a price was exacted for occupying the White House." Where Coolidge had coped with his mother's death through careful, dogged achievement, the loss of his son seemed to deflate his proudest triumph. "When he went," Coolidge wrote in his autobiography, "the power and the glory of the presidency went with him."[12]

. . .

Even if Coolidge had not suffered such a loss, he probably would not have stumped aggressively for president in 1924. Although speaking tours for presidential candidates were no longer as taboo as they had once been, most incumbent presidents of the era— McKinley, Roosevelt, Taft, Wilson—had campaigned in a limited fashion. Averse by temperament to mingling with the hordes, further disposed by Calvin Jr.'s death to withdraw from the public eye, Coolidge found an alternative to public touring in the new broadcast media of radio and newsreels, which he used to burnish his Silent Cal image with the public at large.

In truth, Coolidge's public relations campaign had never stopped. No sooner had Harding been interred in August 1923 than Bruce Barton was back at work penning admiring profiles of the new president for the nation's leading magazines. That September Barton published in the *American Review of Reviews* another formulaic paean extolling Coolidge's Yankee humility and common sense ("Doing the Work and Forgetting About the Credit," "Honesty and Courage in Dealing with the Public"). In December, as Coolidge made his bid for the nomination official, Barton outlined a strategy of magazine stories—including some of Grace Coolidge in the women's magazines—preconvention advertising, and publicity. Barton discerned the new importance of personality in national politics. "This is not a party campaign in the old sense," he noted. "I have not met anybody who is going to vote for the Republican Party. They are going to vote 'for Coolidge' or against him." Accordingly, Barton drew up pamphlets with hokey but effective themes such as "The Farmer Boy, The Public Servant, The President." And he contracted with Charles Scribner's Sons for a sequel to *Have Faith in Massachusetts*—a collection of Coolidge's pre-presidential speeches entitled *The Price of Freedom*.[13]

The president's aides also had a novel tool at their disposal in 1924: radio. Although Coolidge didn't listen to radio much, he used it more effectively than any of his contemporaries. As early as November 1923, Eugene McDonald, the president of the National Association of Broadcasters, a newly formed trade group, urged the president to exploit the fledgling medium. Not only would speaking on the radio spare Coolidge the ordeal of traveling—an ordeal, McDonald suggested, that had felled Harding—it would also allow the president to remake the presidency. "Radio will draw you close to the American fireside for you will be speaking to people as they sit in their living room," McDonald wrote, in language that presaged Franklin Roosevelt's Fireside Chats. "Your voice and your personality will become familiar to them and in consequence . . . you will mean more to them than now." Barton as well insisted that radio had "made possible an entirely new type of campaign" that "enables the president to sit by every fireside and talk in terms of that home's interest and prosperity."[14]

Coolidge's embrace of radio underscored, rather than undermined, his Silent Cal image. Because he could count on his remarks reaching audiences of unprecedented size, he could otherwise retain his customary and effective posture of virtuous reticence. His "reputation is built," his aide Ted Clark explained, "on his habit of keeping silent unless he has some definite idea to get across. . . . The country . . . likes his silence, and it would be a dangerous thing to tear down the picture which they have built." As Coolidge himself told reporters, "I don't recall any candidate for president that ever injured himself very much by not talking." In the campaign, Coolidge gave markedly fewer addresses than Davis or La Follette, but radio and the platform of the presidency guaranteed that his speeches were noticed.[15]

After his 1923 State of the Union message, Coolidge began to give speeches regularly on the radio. He didn't draft remarks expressly for the new medium, as Franklin Roosevelt later would, but arranged to broadcast talks that he was already planning to deliver to live crowds. Otherwise, Coolidge grasped radio's novel benefits. Most obviously, he could command audiences that already numbered in the tens of millions. (Theodore Roosevelt, in contrast, reached perhaps 13 million people with all the speeches he ever gave.) Recognizing the special requirements of addressing large, diverse audiences, Coolidge typically chose to air the talks he gave to nonpartisan forums, at which he delivered statesmanlike speeches, saving more partisan remarks for targeted groups off the air. Some speeches were recorded and distributed on phonograph records as well.[16]

Coolidge knew his voice went over well on the new medium. "I am very fortunate I came in with the radio," he reflected. "I can't make an engaging, rousing, or oratorical speech to a crowd . . . but I have a good radio voice and now I can get my messages across . . . without acquainting them with my lack of oratorical ability." Bascom Slemp declared that radio "seemed to have been invented" for the new president. Less partisan sources agreed. Charles Michelson, the Democratic publicity chief, noted that radio softened the "wire edge to his voice," and William Allen White said that "over the radio, he went straight to the popular heart. His radio campaign helped greatly because it is one of the few mediums by which the president always appears with his best foot forward."[17]

In mid-July, the president's political aide William Butler announced that Coolidge wouldn't be stumping around the country but would wage a front-porch campaign, like Harding and McKinley, only this time from the front porch of the White House—and aided by radio and film. "Supplemented by motion pictures showing the president in action," the New York Times reported, "persons identified with the campaign believe that addresses by

President Coolidge, broadcast throughout the country, would prove a great attraction even to audiences that do not ordinarily go to political meetings."[18]

On August 14, two months after the Republican convention, Coolidge took to the airwaves to accept the GOP nomination, in keeping with the custom of the day. (Not until FDR changed the practice in 1932 did nominees address the convention itself.) A crowd of more than 2,000 people crammed into Washington's Constitution Hall, while another 10,000 massed outside, listening to the speech on loudspeakers. But the main audience—some 25 million—sat in living rooms from the Atlantic to the Rockies and beyond, listening on fifteen networks. The president outlined the economic progress the nation had made over the previous four years, touted the immigration quotas, the Dawes Plan, and his tax cuts, and preached his standard message of stability, prosperity, and industry.[19]

Editorialists on both sides of the aisle heard the speech as an expression of Coolidge's character: straightforward and full of common sense to admirers; cool and uninspired to critics. But the mere fact that Coolidge's personality was now the focus of the campaign represented a triumph for the president. "We might as well recognize frankly that we have nothing to sell but Calvin Coolidge," Barton wrote to George Barr Baker, a journalist turned GOP publicist, in July. The statement contained more confidence than concern, for Calvin Coolidge, as the public understood him, was a sturdy product.[20]

Throughout the summer the focus remained on Coolidge personally. When the president went to Plymouth Notch to visit his son's grave and to escape Washington, Barton made sure that reporters and cameras recorded him in his native setting. Coolidge chopped trees and pitched hay in his business suit and homburg, as Henry Ford, Thomas Edison, and Harvey Firestone—longtime "camping pals," according to the papers—journeyed to Vermont for a publicity stunt. The businessmen sat with Coolidge in a Gloucester hammock on his veranda and sang his praises for reporters, while the president gave Ford a sap bucket that had belonged to his great-great-grandfather John Coolidge, the first of his line to settle in Plymouth. The predictable headlines followed.[21]

The Silent Cal strategy generally seemed to be succeeding. But one flaw was that Coolidge's shyness could also make him seem chilly or unappealing to voters. So the president undertook to calibrate his persona. Besides Barton, he brought in another leading public relations man of the day, Edward Bernays, the nephew of the great psychoanalyst Sigmund Freud, to help humanize him in the public eye. More liberal politically than Barton, Bernays also took a different view of publicity. Where Barton emphasized the appeal of the ordinary, Bernays stressed the extraordinary; where Barton's gimmicks tended to reassure audiences, Bernays sought to excite them.

Bernays convinced Coolidge to host a breakfast with a gaggle of entertainers—in those days mostly Republicans—including the wildly popular vaudeville artist and blackface performer Al Jolson. On an October morning, thirty actors showed up at the White House after an all-night train ride from New York for what the *New York Times*, showing itself vulnerable to the public relations men's craft, described as "an old New England breakfast of sausage and hot cakes." Afterward, Jolson led the guests in a song, "Keep Coolidge!" in which he trilled: "The race is now begun / And Coolidge is the one / The one to fill the presidential chair." The next day, the *Times* headline marveled: "Actors Eat Cakes with Coolidge . . . President Nearly Laughs." As Bernays later reflected, "The country felt that a man in the White House who could laugh with Al Jolson and the Dolly sisters was not frigid and unsympathetic."[22]

Bernays did some other work for the president, too. He joined forces with Rhinelander Waldo, a former police commissioner of New York City and a Coolidge admirer, in creating a front group called the Coolidge Non-Partisan League, which would showcase prominent Democrats as well as Republicans who favored the incumbent. In later times, boasting of testimonials from the other party would become a tried-and-true campaign technique, but in 1924 it still had considerable novelty. Barton, for his part, pre-scribed a tactic used in cosmetics advertising called testimonials, in which average Americans would mouth seemingly spontaneous praise for the president. "We will build up a wonderful Coolidge legend in the country," he gushed. "Emotions affect votes much more than logic. I am sure of the soundness of this plan."[23]

As the election neared, Coolidge took to the radio regularly. "We literally filled the air with Republican addresses from the various studios during the entire month of October," crowed John Tilson of the Republican Party's speakers' bureau. Coolidge gave a speech to the U.S. Chamber of Commerce on October 23 that was broadcast nationally and another radio address the night before Election Day. Carried on a coast-to-coast hookup, the latter speech attracted an audience greater than any other speaker had ever enjoyed. Playing to the exhilaration about the event's novelty, Coolidge paid tribute to his whole audience "including my father, up on the Vermont farm, listening in." The journalist Bruce Bliven noted, "Calvin Coolidge's speeches have been heard by at least ten times as many people as have heard any other man who ever lived." This fact alone, he suggested, provided hundreds of thousands of voters with "a link between themselves and the White House and a powerful reason to vote in his favor."[24]

Some found all the theatrics a bit much. At a time when cultural critics were awakening to the power of propaganda—and question-ing its implications for democracy—several accused the president of perpetrating a massive snow job. "The American people dearly love to be fooled," the *Nation* lamented, "to worship politicians of whom they have created portraits which bear little or no resem-blance to the originals." Its editors asserted that "the Coolidge myth has been created by amazingly skillful propaganda." Bliven con-tended that Coolidge was sold "as though he were a new breakfast food or fountain pen"—a campaign in which "the Republican National Committee had the whole-hearted aid of the editors, film producers, etc., to an extent which was likewise without any parallel in our history." Such complaints, however, remained confined largely to journalists and intellectuals. Coolidge could rest confident that most Americans perceived him as sincere and true.[25]

•   •   •

Ironically, publicity innovations may not have been necessary to reelect Coolidge. With labor radicalism diminishing, business improving, and even farmers enjoying a brief uptick in their incomes, Coolidge could stick to the kind of ground game that suited his temperament. "If you keep as much as you can to an expression of general principles, rather than attempting to go into particular details of legislation," he advised Dawes, who was stumping for the ticket, "you will save yourself from a great deal of annoying criticism." (He added: "P.S. Whenever you go anywhere, take Mrs. Dawes along.") The absence of a record of legislative achievement like Wilson's or of executive dynamism like Roosevelt's seemed to bother relatively few voters. The $4.3 million Republican Party war chest, which dwarfed the Democrats' $820,000, didn't hurt either.[26]

La Follette's presence in the race, moreover, helped Coolidge substantially. The Republicans attacked the Wisconsin Progressive more than they did the hapless Davis. Since the Red Scare of 1919 and 1920, fear of Bolshevism had cooled considerably, and Coolidge had even softened the hard line against recognizing the Communist regime in Russia. But assailing La Follette's radicalism, even to the point of fearmongering, proved irresistible. "Whether America will allow itself to be degraded into a communistic or socialistic state, or whether it will remain American," said the president, loomed as the signal issue in the campaign. "Coolidge or Chaos" became the Republicans' rallying cry, with the sober, even-keeled president offering himself as a rock of stability in changing times. Oswald Garrison Villard, the editor of the *Nation*, explained that Americans seemed to feel that Coolidge "is just what the country needs, a quiet, simple, unobtrusive man, with no isms and no desire for any reform." Coolidge even managed to rally to his side a number of prominent liberals. In October, the *New Republic* ran a debate among its contributors over whom to vote for. While the liberal thinkers Herbert Croly and Felix Frankfurter backed La Follette and Walter Lippmann came out for Davis, Chester Rowell, a longtime progressive, maintained that he and other onetime Theodore Roosevelt supporters "are now for Coolidge" because of their "confidence in his personal independence of reactionary influence."[27]

Coolidge had done an exceptional job of mastering the new methods of politics in a mass society. Just as in his statements on the veterans' bonus and tax cuts he had invoked his belief in a common good that trumped minority interests, so in his campaigning he had held himself out as a tribune of the American people writ large. To his loyal aide Bascom Slemp, the appeal to the majority was undeniable. "From his lips fell his declaration of policy, drawled in the tang of Vermont, with no grace of delivery or art of oratory, but so profound and true that it captured and held the minds of men," he wrote. "In eighteen months he had a unanimity of following in the country rare in our political history." More objectively, Kenneth Roberts of the *Saturday Evening Post* noted, "The Coolidge political machine to all intents and purposes has always been a one-man machine, and the one man has been Calvin Coolidge."[28]

On November 4, Coolidge and Dawes were elected in another Republican landslide. The president won 15 million votes—more than Davis's 8 million and La Follette's 4.8 million combined. (La Follette's 17 percent of the vote was a strong showing, historically, for a third-party candidate.) Thirty-five states cast 382 electoral votes for Coolidge, with Davis winning only the former Confederate states and Oklahoma. Davis garnered the lowest percentage of the vote of any Democrat ever. Even the historically low turnout—only 48.9 percent of eligible voters showed up at the polls, a dramatic contrast to the high percentages of the late nineteenth century—revealed at worst a lack of burning discontent with the incumbent. In the Congress, the Republicans bolstered their majorities, gaining

four seats in the Senate and twenty-two in the House. Yet as Bruce
Bliven would later note, "The election of 1924 is now universally
admitted to have been not a Republican victory but a Coolidge triumph." As such, it would mean a second term in which the president's personal popularity would remain high but his opportunities
to produce far-reaching changes would remain few.[29]

8

Beyond America's Shores

On March 4, 1925, a clear, mild day in Washington, Calvin Coolidge took his second oath of office. The day was a study in self-effacement. The president's speech was unmemorable, historic only as another first in radio broadcasting. He was upstaged, in fact, by Dawes, his irrepressible vice president, who in his maiden speech surprised the senators of whom he was now the nominal leader by urging them to reform their antiquated rules of debate, which he called "inimical . . . to the principles of our constitutional government." Coolidge's parsimony, meanwhile, put a damper on the lunchtime festivities. Instead of hosting the usual feast, the Coolidges lunched on sandwiches with the Daweses in private while cabinet officers and dignitaries stood around in the White House Blue Room, baffled. Eventually, a military officer invited the crowd to join in a buffet next door at the State, War, and Navy Building, and thus when Coolidge and Dawes eventually descended from their meal, the entourage had disappeared.[1]

Coolidge's big victory in November and the Republican gains in Congress should have improved his prospects on Capitol Hill. The death in November of Henry Cabot Lodge, the Republican Senate leader, also should have smoothed relations—especially because Coolidge saw to it that his ally William Butler was picked to serve out Lodge's term. Nonetheless Coolidge again ran into trouble, starting with that potential pitfall of all new administrations, his appointments.

Even before his new term began, Coolidge had a vacancy to fill on the Supreme Court. Justice Joseph McKenna, eighty-one years old and nearly senile after a stroke several years earlier, finally retired. According to Nicholas Murray Butler, the president considered nominating the New York jurist Benjamin Cardozo to replace McKenna but concluded that with one Jew on the Court already (Louis Brandeis) the choice of a second "would excite criticism." Instead, Coolidge nominated his old Amherst chum and well-regarded attorney general Harlan Fiske Stone.[2]

Praised in the legal world and in the press, the Stone nomination should have sailed through the Senate. But as attorney general Stone was carrying out a politically motivated investigation of Senator Burton Wheeler, which Harding's attorney general Harry Daugherty had vengefully initiated back during the Teapot Dome scandal when Wheeler was clamoring for Daugherty's head. Foolishly (or courageously), Stone sought an indictment of Wheeler on the eve of his own confirmation vote.

Wheeler, Thomas Walsh, George Norris, and a few other farm bloc senators went after Stone, both for retaining Daugherty's men at Justice and for his own Wall Street ties. For the first time in history, a High Court nominee had to appear personally before the Senate Judiciary Committee, where his antagonists grilled him. Ultimately, however, the westerners' obstreperousness came across as political, and Stone was confirmed, 71 to 6. He would go on to a distinguished term on the Court, where he became an important voice upholding the constitutionality of the New Deal, and Franklin Roosevelt would name him chief justice in 1941. (Wheeler, for his part, was acquitted.) Nonetheless, the fracas showed Coolidge that his mandate with the public wouldn't give him the free hand on the Hill that he had lacked in his first term.

Coolidge stumbled again when, on Inauguration Day, he chose Charles Warren of Michigan to replace Stone as attorney general. A lawyer, businessman, and former ambassador to Japan and Mexico, Warren was disliked by many fellow Republicans for his arrogance. More troubling, his work as counsel to the Michigan Sugar Company, which was under investigation for antitrust practices, made him ethically suspect. Given the administration's reputation for serving big business, the choice was ill considered.

Coolidge hadn't consulted with party leaders on the pick, and his allies on the Hill managed the nomination poorly. Convinced they had the votes they needed, they neither actively addressed the ethical concerns nor carefully planned their floor strategy. Even Edmund Starling, having heard that Warren was in trouble, tried to warn Coolidge, but the president grew testy. "Well," he snapped, "you're such a great Secret Service man I guess you know more than anybody else. You know everything." Then, on March 9, during the Senate's debate on the nomination, Republican floor leader Charles Curtis feared he was losing support and called the roll without the full Senate in attendance. It soon became clear that the senators present would split down the middle, 40–40. Normally, the vice president would break the tie, but Dawes had gone to his Willard Hotel room for a nap. Summoned, he hurried over in a taxicab but arrived too late to vote, and Warren's nomination was defeated—the first time the Senate had rejected a cabinet appointee since 1868.[3]

Coolidge was furious. "I hesitate a good deal to subject anyone I might appoint to any such ordeal as confronted Mr. Warren," he sniffed to reporters. He refused to accept defeat. He talked of temporarily appointing Warren, as was his constitutional prerogative, while Congress was in recess. Leaning on his Senate loyalists for help, he renominated Warren and got another vote. But on March 18, the Senate rejected Warren again, this time by a decisive margin, 46 to 39—a slap at the president, who had raised the stakes. Coolidge was distraught; Starling watched him, upon learning the news, take a curtain cord from the Oval Office anteroom and absently tie it into knots. Abandoning the idea of a recess appointment, Coolidge instead chose a lifelong friend, John Sargent of Plymouth Notch, a former attorney general of Vermont, for the position. Sargent passed unanimously and without delay.[4]

Coolidge's other new appointments went smoothly. Hughes's retirement from State left the biggest shoes to fill; to succeed him Coolidge chose Frank Kellogg, a contemporary and friend of Theodore Roosevelt, a former senator from Minnesota, and the ambassador to Great Britain. Though sixty-nine and blind in one eye, Kellogg had the stature, if not the skill, to replace Hughes. At Agriculture William Jardine of Kansas filled the seat of Henry Wallace Sr., who had died the previous autumn. Bascom Slemp, unable to persuade Coolidge to give him a cabinet post, stepped down, and former representative Everett Sanders of Indiana took his place as chief White House aide.

A final decision of note was the retention of Herbert Hoover as secretary of commerce. Hoover was a perpetual rival of the president's. Both men had been dark horse candidates for the GOP nomination in 1920, and before Coolidge ascended to the presidency in August 1923, Hoover's name had been floated for the 1924 nod as well. He was also in many ways Coolidge's stylistic opposite. A Stanford-trained engineer who had heroically supervised food relief efforts for war-torn Europe, Hoover was a workaholic, policy wonk, and hands-on manger. As commerce secretary, he was forever seeking ways to reduce waste throughout the private sector. Coolidge viewed Hoover's ambition and ostentatious activism—as well as his insatiable appetite for publicity—with scorn, and he privately labeled him "Wonder Boy." But the president also knew that Hoover's penchant for taking on projects meshed perfectly with his own practice of delegation. "I cannot tell you how many things I feel we are dependent on you about," Slemp told Hoover in December 1923. (Nor were all these things policy matters; with his California ties, Hoover helped Coolidge quash Hiram Johnson's bid for the 1924 GOP nomination by bringing the Golden State delegation into line behind the president.) In Coolidge's second term, Hoover would spearhead many of the administration's most prominent initiatives—from bringing water to the interior West to coordinating relief after the ruinous 1927 Mississippi flood—as he plotted his own run for the presidency in 1928. "Except in the newspapers and the political field," remarked T.R.B. of the *New Republic,* "there is more Hoover in the administration than there is Coolidge." Seeing the wisdom in retaining Hoover, Coolidge nonetheless eyed him warily.[5]

• • •

Hoover's activism would, at least initially, take a backseat to developments abroad that claimed the president's attention as his second term opened. Coolidge turned to foreign affairs with reluctance. Here, as with other matters, he liked to delegate, rather than dictating policy himself. Regarding his China policy, he once told Undersecretary of State Joseph Grew, "I don't know anything about this. You do, Mr. Grew, and you're in charge. You settle the problem, and I'll back you up." Another time he told Mellon, as the Treasury secretary set sail for Europe, to tell all inquirers that "their problems should properly be taken up through regular diplomatic channels."[6]

The delegation created the appearance of indifference. Elihu Root, Theodore Roosevelt's secretary of state, moaned that Coolidge "did not have an international hair on his head." He ultimately declined to recognize the Communist government of the Soviet Union, and his policy toward the internal strife and rising anti-Western sentiment in China was uncertain and reactive. Coolidge, however, was no isolationist. Rather, his cautious temperament disinclined him from making bold ventures. He governed, moreover, at a moment when the public had lost its patience for the swashbuckling of a Roosevelt or the internationalism of a Wilson. Indeed, the president's critics on foreign affairs were mainly those men who distrusted his internationalist forays altogether, from the Dawes Plan in his first term to his efforts to join the World Court in his second. He was fighting isolationism, not carrying its banner.

The question of the World Court, formally known as the Permanent Court of International Justice, came to the fore early in

Coolidge's second term. Since the body's formation in 1922, the issue of American membership had loomed large. The nations of Europe, recoiling from the horror of World War I, hoped that the court, as a judicial arm of the League of Nations, would help them settle their conflicts peacefully. But in the United States, politics had been convulsed less by the war itself than by Wilson's failure to secure American membership in the league. Thus, where European leaders looked to forge a sense of collective security, American leaders feared running afoul of popular isolationist feeling. By Coolidge's presidency, pacifist Progressives and Main Street Republicans allied to snuff out any talk of joining the League. "The incident, so far as we are concerned, is closed," Coolidge conceded in his 1923 State of the Union address.[7]

Joining the World Court was another matter. The body, which sat at The Hague in the Netherlands, comprised a panel of arbiters who adjudicated disputes among nations. Republican eminences such as Elihu Root and William Howard Taft had come to see international law, rooted in principles and dispensed by impartial judges, as a more stable and fair guarantor of peace than diplomacy, which could change with new administrations and new players and was full of intrigue. Following such thinking, President Harding had called for America to join the World Court, and Coolidge repeated the plea. "The proposal," he said, "presents the only practical plan on which many nations have agreed, though it may not meet every desire."[8]

At first Coolidge pressed his case lightly. Although Lodge was dead, William Borah, who had taken the reins of the Senate Foreign Relations Committee, was equally stout in his opposition to the court, and Hughes and Coolidge feared taking on the powerful Idahoan. The president rationalized his inaction to Theodore Roosevelt Jr., now occupying his father's old post of assistant secretary of the navy: "My predecessor submitted it to the Senate. No action is called for, therefore, by me as an executive."[9]

During the 1924 campaign, however, Coolidge reiterated his desire to join the World Court, and his new term offered another chance to persuade Borah and the so-called Irreconcilables to temper their fierce jealousy of American sovereignty. In a post-election message to Congress, Coolidge again called for the United States to join the body while pledging that "our country shall not be bound by advisory opinions which may be rendered by the Court upon questions which we have not voluntarily submitted for its judgment." Although the Senate declined to take up the issue in its winter session of 1924–25, in March the House of Representatives, in a symbolic but powerful gesture, approved American membership by a whopping margin of 303 to 28. Coolidge took up the matter again in his March inaugural.[10]

It was a new player in the drama, Frank Kellogg, who kept the issue alive. In his first official statement as secretary of state, on April 25, 1925, Kellogg firmly backed membership with words that reflected the enlightened opinion of the age: "Is it not time that the conscience of the world should inculcate in the minds of the people a better way to settle disputes than by going to war?" Emboldened by public support of membership, Coolidge pressed the matter himself, declaring, "I can conceive of nothing that we could do, which involves assuming so few obligations on our part, that would likely prove to be of so much value to the world." Nudged by public opinion, senators too looked for ways to support a modified protocol.[11]

Finally, on January 26, 1926, in a 76–17 vote that crossed party lines, the Senate approved the protocol with the required two-thirds supermajority. But the protocol carried amendments that limited the court's jurisdiction over the United States and stipulated that by joining the court the United States would not be also joining the League of Nations. Many pro-court senators supported these provisions in order to garner the needed votes—as did Coolidge. "It will be regarded all over the world as a helpful attitude," he predicted of the Senate's action, "and an expression of the sentiment of desiring to cooperate." But the provisions turned out to be poison pills. "I believe with the reservations that it carries," South Dakota's Peter Norbeck pronounced with satisfaction, "that it is entirely harmless, if not helpless."[12]

World Court members, led by Britain, immediately made clear

their skepticism of the Senate's tinkering. It was now incumbent on Coolidge, if he was serious about joining, to sway European opinion. Yet he failed to do so. Before the National Press Club in April, he expressed his satisfaction with the Senate's problematic amendments, and he declined an invitation from the League of Nations to discuss the outstanding issues. "Of course, it was a most courteous thing for the League to do," he told reporters, before adding matter-of-factly, "I don't see any necessity for any discussion on our part." Coolidge feared giving domestic critics new grounds for claiming that court membership was a prelude to submission to world governance. But his caution would be his undoing. In September 1926, a conference of court signatories gathered in Geneva to consider the Americans' "special conditions." But Coolidge had given them little reason to accept the Senate's terms. Rather than spurning the United States outright, they put the ball back in Coolidge's court by consenting to the terms but with modifications of their own— modifications that the already balking Senate would find hard to swallow.[13]

Coolidge still refused to budge. For all the enthusiasm he had shown the year before, he now seemed fatalistic about the irreconcilability of the court signatories' stand and the Senate's—which he gave no reason to believe differed from his own. Even pro-court voices at home concluded, with the *New York Herald Tribune*, that America "could not accept membership at the Geneva Conference's price."[14]

Coolidge made his position clear on November 11, after the midterm elections. Having failed to bring the European nations around to the Senate's position, he did not ask the Senate to review its January terms. "I do not believe the Senate would take favorable action on any such proposal," he said, "and unless the requirements of the Senate resolution are met, I can see no prospect of this country adhering to the Court." The issue languished for another year, and despite a final effort to revise the protocol led by Elihu Root at the end of Coolidge's term, the United States would not join the

League of Nations World Court under Coolidge—or, for that matter, under any American president. Only after the hard lessons of World War II would the United States join a new world court, reconstituted as part of the United Nations.[15]

. . .

Coolidge faced trouble closer to home as well. The Americas had been a source of both opportunity and irritation for the United States for decades, and since Theodore Roosevelt's time presidents had regularly dispatched the marines to the Caribbean or Central America to depose or shore up various regimes. By Coolidge's day, the United States was more or less managing the affairs of ten Latin American countries. In some countries Coolidge began to repair strained relations—early in his second term, notably, he arranged for the withdrawal of marines from the Dominican Republic—but elsewhere old problems were resurfacing.

One sore spot was Mexico. The latest round of hostilities dated to 1916, when Woodrow Wilson sent troops there in an unsuccessful bid to apprehend the revolutionary leader Pancho Villa; then Mexico, unofficially casting its lot with Germany in World War I, nationalized much land and property—including oil fields—claimed by American companies. When President Alvaro Obregon took office in 1920, the United States refused to recognize his government.

By the time Coolidge became president, however, the situation was improving. During Harding's last months, Hughes had worked to normalize relations between the two countries, and Obregon reciprocated. On September 1, 1923, Coolidge recognized the Obregon administration, and Mexico agreed to compensate Americans whose property had been seized. A few months later, Coolidge strengthened the bond: to help Obregon suppress a revolt, he lifted a weapons embargo and urged American banks to tender loans to Mexico to buy arms. "If we allow Obregon to be overthrown," Coolidge explained, "we shall be put in a ridiculous position as we have already rendered him some aid and are committed to his cause."[16]

The ascension of Plutarco Elias Calles to the Mexican presidency in late 1924 changed the calculus. Unhappy with the 1923 accords, Calles indulged in sharp anti-American rhetoric and in late 1925 restricted American oil and land claims—a move that Coolidge and Kellogg, along with many businessmen, viewed as an illegitimate confiscation of Americans' property. Calles also sought to nationalize the holdings of the Catholic Church, provoking a fight with the bishops of Mexico and prompting American Catholics to join the oil companies in seeking military intervention. Under countervailing pressure from Borah and the Senate, Coolidge and Kellogg resisted. Instead, they tried for the next year to salve tensions with rhetoric, praising the Mexican government's progress in restoring order and minimizing the problems, even as they insisted on indemnity payments for the disputed land.

Compounding matters, the Mexican crisis had become entwined with tensions in another long-standing Latin American trouble spot: Nicaragua. There, too, Coolidge's term had dawned amid hope. American-supervised elections in 1924 had gone well, and "for the first time in many years," Joseph Grew asserted in January 1925, the nation was "in a peaceful and progressive condition." In August, Coolidge withdrew the American troops that had been buttressing Nicaragua's conservative regime since 1912.[17]

When the marines left, however, civil war resumed. By January 1926, the American-backed president had been overthrown by General Emiliano Chamorro, who imposed a military dictatorship. The deposed vice president, Juan Sacasa—a liberal who owed his post to a short-lived power-sharing arrangement—fled to Mexico, where he secured Calles's help in launching an armed effort to regain power.

Coolidge realized he could restore order—and protect American corporate interests—only by sending the marines back in. The USS *Cleveland* landed in May 1926, and Coolidge escalated American involvement over the next months. In November 1926 Chamorro agreed to resign in favor of the pro-American Adolfo Diaz. But Sacasa's liberal forces remained bent on seizing power, and in late

December more marines headed south. "This government is not taking any sides, one way or the other, in relation to the revolution," Coolidge insisted disingenuously.[18]

In 1927 the twin Latin American crises came to a head. In Mexico, the American ambassador, James Sheffield, resigned, having led Coolidge "into a bog," as Bruce Bliven wrote. In July, Coolidge asked his old friend Dwight Morrow to clean up the mess. "My only instructions," he told Morrow, "are to keep us out of war." Morrow came through. Good-natured and freewheeling, he charmed Mexican officials and, with his broken Spanish and trips to the bazaars, endeared himself to the people as well. He brought Charles Lindbergh and Will Rogers to Mexico City, to his host citizens' delight. Within the year, despite some grumbling from American oil companies, he struck a deal with Calles that let American companies keep the rights to lands they had bought before 1917, with leases required for post-1917 acquisitions. Morrow also helped the Calles government negotiate agreements with the Catholic Church and Mexican businesses. A period of good neighborliness followed.[19]

The Nicaraguan problem, however, festered. At the start of 1927 civil war was still raging, and Diaz was far from popular. On January 10, Coolidge delivered a speech to Congress, trying to persuade Borah, Norris, Wheeler, and his other antagonists to support continued military intervention. "There is no question that if the revolution continues, American investments and business interests in Nicaragua will be very seriously affected, if not destroyed," Coolidge said candidly. The senators balked; Coolidge sent more marines anyway.[20]

But congressional pressure led Coolidge to pursue other avenues as well. Again the turning point came when the president chose a high-profile diplomat to mediate, in this case the august former secretary of war Henry Stimson. "If you find a chance to straighten the matter out," Coolidge told him, in a tone similar to that which he used with Morrow, "I want you to do so." Arriving in Nicaragua in April, Stimson adopted a stance akin to Morrow's: the confident gentleman diplomat mixing charm and muscle. Within weeks, he coaxed the combatants into a coalition government. New elections were scheduled for 1928 and 1932, under American supervision, and United States troops would be withdrawn by 1933. Stimson and Coolidge claimed victory.[21]

In this case, however, the resolution was illusory. Although the November 1928 election came off more or less as hoped, with the liberal Jose Moncada prevailing, peace didn't last. General Augusto Cesar Sandino, previously aligned with Sacasa, rejected the Stimson agreements, took to the jungles, led a prolonged insurrection, and killed a handful of marines and thousands of Nicaraguans. After several years of continued warfare, the U.S.–backed government and its National Guard, led by Anastasio Somoza, had Sandino assassinated in 1934. The wars between the Somozas and the Sandinistas would fester for decades.

Indeed, despite short-term gains, Coolidge had in the end done little to address the core problem in the hemisphere: for all their eagerness to attract investment, Latin Americans viewed the United States as an imperial power. Thus, U.S.–backed regimes were inherently unstable, while those that sought to redistribute land and wealth invariably incurred American suspicion. Coolidge's interventions, though restrained in contrast to those of some presidents, still amounted to meddling, especially since he barely concealed the goal of protecting American business interests. For Coolidge, the chief business of empire was business.

The hemisphere's simmering anti-Americanism erupted at the Sixth Annual International Conference of American States in Havana in January 1928. Leaving the United States for only the second time in his life, Coolidge delivered the keynote address, arguing that the American nations shared common values and goals. But Coolidge's overture—the first trip by a sitting president to Cuba— couldn't suppress long-standing resentments. After his departure, Mexico, El Salvador, and Argentina proposed a resolution, clearly directed at the United States, denying the right of any state to "intervene in the internal affairs of another." One delegation after another rose to offer support for the resolution, while Charles

Evans Hughes, representing the United States as a special envoy, squirmed. When his turn came, Hughes mustered a tour de force of a speech that convinced the Salvadoran delegate to withdraw the divisive resolution. But the issue of American imperialism had been broached.[22]

After the conference, Kellogg had his legal adviser draft a white paper that advised against direct military intervention in Latin America, arguing for other methods of maintaining hemispheric influence. The paper never became official policy but it did signal that, as Coolidge's presidency waned, the State Department was starting to take anti-Americanism seriously. Soon the United States would be inching toward the "Good Neighbor Policy" of Franklin Roosevelt. The Coolidge crises, in bringing Latin American discontent to a head, had the small saving grace of helping to clarify the need for a less imperialistic policy.

• • •

This shift in Latin American policy was of a piece with the growing postwar desire among the world's powers to erect structures to promote world peace. If Coolidge could not (or would not) join the League of Nations or the World Court, he was keen to pursue arms control.

Again, Coolidge followed Harding's path. In 1921–22, Secretary of State Hughes had convened the Washington Conference on International Disarmament. Those parleys produced three treaties, signed by nine world powers, that capped the number of their battleships, aircraft carriers, and naval armaments. Although Coolidge wished to continue the arms limitation process, it wasn't until the fall of 1926 that he committed himself to the effort. One unforeseen result of limiting battleships and carriers in 1922 had been renewed competition to build another class of warship, cruisers, whose development remained unchecked. Thus in February 1927 Coolidge called for a June conference in Geneva aimed at limiting these vessels as well.[23]

The gathering got off to a poor start. France and Italy declined to participate, leaving only the United States, Britain, and Japan to negotiate. Moreover, America's relative paucity of existing cruisers made its demands for caps on these ships sound self-serving. Japan and Britain, for their part, failed to surmount their fears about restricting their own defenses. Coolidge's conference thus concluded in August with no new treaties. The failure provoked pointed criticism of the president and his international leadership. In the budget he unveiled in December, he called for a huge increase in naval building—a departure from his fiscal discipline and a concession that a naval arms treaty was not to be.

Geneva's failure, however, gave a boost to another campaign that sought something even more ambitious than arms limits: outlawing war altogether. For years an assortment of domestic peace activists had been championing an international pact that would commit its signatories to renouncing military aggression as a national policy. Only peaceful means, they hoped, would be used to solve international disputes.

The "outlawry of war," as it was called, had its roots in the revulsion against the horrors of World War I and gathered a strong grassroots following throughout the 1920s. In March 1927, James Shotwell, a prominent Columbia University professor and leading advocate, visited France, where he pitched his ideas to the French foreign minister, Aristide Briand. France had just sat out the Geneva Conference, and Briand saw an opportunity to repair relations with the United States while gaining an American pledge to secure the existing boundaries in Europe. On April 6, he endorsed the idea of a bilateral treaty, and the movement gathered momentum.

Initially, Coolidge and Kellogg remained cool to the scheme. They distrusted Briand's motives and found the whole idea naive. "There isn't any shortcut to peace," Coolidge told reporters. But the peace activists and editorialists, having lost on the League of Nations and the World Court and seen the Geneva Conference fizzle, ratcheted up the pressure. Senate Foreign Relations Committee chairman William Borah threw his weight behind the idea—an important push, since the Idahoan spoke for the many Americans who opposed the League of Nations and the World Court as foreign entanglements yet loftily sought peace. Borah also insisted that any treaty encompass more than just the United States and France; a bilateral treaty would put the signatories at a disadvantage relative to other world powers, he maintained, whereas a comprehensive pact would not. In December 1927, Coolidge and Kellogg endorsed this more palatable version of the proposal, which also solved the problem of seeming to forge a special bond with France.[24]

Soon one nation after another was voicing its enthusiasm for the pact. Coolidge agreed to send Kellogg to Paris to sign the treaty, although he continued to express some skepticism. "I do not especially like the meeting that is to be held in Paris," he said. "While it is ostensibly to sign the treaty, I cannot help wondering whether it may not be for some other purpose not yet disclosed." Eventually the president, sensing the public mood, surmounted his doubts. On August 27, 1928, the United States joined fourteen other nations in signing the Kellogg-Briand Pact in Paris, outlawing war as an instrument of national policy.[25]

Ratification came next. Coolidge knew he couldn't afford to lose another Senate battle. Although his term was winding down, he desired a political victory to go out on. Britain and France spoke of attaching reservations to the treaty, but Coolidge resisted the temptation. Instead he impressed on Congress the urgency of ratifying what he called "one of the most important treaties ever laid before the Senate of the United States." Showing an unwonted knack for working the Senate, he deployed Kellogg and Dawes to sway wavering senators and even lobbied lawmakers himself. Ultimately, he prevailed, on a vote of 85 to 1, in January 1929, shortly before he left office.[26]

By 1933, another forty-nine countries had signed the Kellogg-Briand Pact. Following Dawes, Kellogg became the second Coolidge administration official to win a Nobel Peace Prize. Others, however, derided the pact as "worthless, but harmless." In the long run, the naysayers proved to be correct. The Nazi regime would shred the pact, along with the Locarno agreement and every other treaty the Weimar German government had signed. Ironically, in the case of a rare congressional and diplomatic victory, Coolidge's initial instincts were right. There was no shortcut to peace.[27]

9

High Tide of Republicanism

In the spring of 1927, Calvin Coolidge's presidency appeared to be at high tide. On the global stage, the president was inching the country and the world's powers closer toward the goal of lasting peace. At home, prosperity was in full swing, the middle class rising. If Americans were complacent about politics, it was a complacency at least partly born of contentment. The New Era had dawned. Or so, at any rate, it seemed.

No act of daring gave better expression to Americans' buoyant confidence than the thirty-three-and-a-half-hour transatlantic flight of Charles Augustus Lindbergh. Lindbergh's solo journey from New York to Paris on May 20–21, 1927, transformed the blond, twenty-five-year-old aviator into a folk hero. Showered with awards and parades, named *Time* magazine's first "Man of the Year," Lindbergh was a product of the new cult of celebrity, an emblem of the age.

For Coolidge, Lindbergh's was a triumph not just to admire but also to exploit. Calls arose for the pilot to be given his own postage stamp (which he got), his own holiday (which he got, after a fashion, when the day of his return was deemed a national day of celebration), and a permanent waiver from paying federal income taxes (with which he had—the Mellon tax plan notwithstanding—no such luck). Coolidge hastened to receive Lindbergh in Washington with suitable fanfare. Because the president was scheduled to leave on June 13 for the Black Hills of South Dakota—like most presidents, Coolidge vacated Washington for much of the sweltering summer— he had Secretary of State Frank Kellogg cable Lindbergh to cut short his European victory lap so the president could personally greet the aviator in Washington on June 11.

Coolidge arranged a grand welcome. A navy cruiser ferried the pilot and his plane home from Europe. Once they neared the American shore, they were joined by an escort of four destroyers, twenty-seven fighter planes, and a dirigible. Former secretary of state Charles Evans Hughes and three cabinet members greeted Lindbergh at the Navy Yard in Washington. Next came a parade to the Washington Monument, watched by 300,000 Americans who had poured into the nation's capital and heard by a record 30 million listening to what the *New York Times* called "the greatest hook-up in radio history."[1]

The festivities culminated in a midday speech by the president, his "most impressive address," according to the journalist Charles Merz, "since his annual message to Congress" in 1923. Some 150,000 spectators gathered, many of them camped out on the Mall for hours under the hottest sun of the year. (Unfortunately, many government employees couldn't attend since Coolidge refused to declare an official holiday, explaining that he had already extended too many half-holidays to federal workers.) At the Mall, the president spoke about "this genial, modest American youth" who was "driven by an unconquerable will and inspired by the imagination and the spirit of his Viking ancestors." He promoted Lindbergh, a mere National Guard captain, to the rank of colonel in the Army Reserve Corps and awarded him the Distinguished Flying Cross. The filmmaker Lee De Forest recorded the sights and sounds for showings in a Washington theater.[2]

The Lindbergh fete continued with a late lunch and, that night, a dinner that Coolidge hosted in the mansion of the newspaper mogul Eleanor "Cissy" Patterson, where the president was staying while the White House underwent renovations. At lunch, the men were joined by Dwight Morrow, on the verge of his mission to Mexico. (Lindbergh would forge a friendship with Morrow and later marry his daughter Anne.) After dinner, a crowd of some seven thousand congregated outside the Patterson mansion, chanting, "We want Lindy!" until the aviator poked his head out a library window and bowed to his admirers. The next morning the pilot joined the Coolidges at Sunday services, which were moved to the Metropolitan Theater to accommodate a crowd of 2,000 suddenly devout Congregationalists.[3]

On Monday Coolidge decamped to the Black Hills and Lindbergh to New York, where an even bigger party awaited him. Yet for all the glory that Lindbergh would reap—the sacks of telegrams, the reams of doggerel, the dance craze bearing his name—the phenomenon of his adoration was about more than one man's heroism. He was, declared one pundit after another, a "symbol" of America who told its people something about themselves. In the Lindbergh revelry of 1927, Americans were really throwing themselves a party for fighting past the disillusionment and hard times of the postwar years and into the New Era—without, they were starting to believe, losing their souls. Lindbergh, wrote the journalist Mary Mullet, "has shown us that we are not rotten at the core, but morally sound and sweet and good." Years later, Lindbergh would be revealed as an anti-Semite and Nazi sympathizer—and later still, as the father of illegitimate children. Yet when the young flier burst on the scene in 1927, the public swooned over his professed humility and moderation. It was for showing that the old-fashioned American qualities of modesty, restraint, and self-reliance could survive in the modern, kinetic 1920s that Americans celebrated him so lavishly.[4]

They could just as well have been celebrating Calvin Coolidge.

• • •

Even before Lindbergh's feat, Coolidge had reason to think his presidency was going well. Although he never tamed Congress, in 1926 he had succeeded in pushing through another slice of the Mellon program—the proudest achievement of his presidency.

Having secured only a scaled-back bill in 1924, the president felt emboldened after his election victory to try again.

The 1926 Mellon bill provided for across-the-board income tax cuts, zeroed out the gift tax, halved the estate tax, and slashed sur-taxes on the wealthy to 20 percent. Supporting it were several trade associations, banks, local chambers of commerce, and a business lobby formerly called the American Bankers' League, which had renamed itself the American Taxpayers' League. The Democrats, adrift and cowed by their 1924 election losses, folded their hand; Senator Furnifold Simmons, one of Coolidge's chief antagonists from 1924, backed the new bill, he said, "to make businessmen real-ize that the Democratic Party is not bent on taxing them or their enterprises exorbitantly." And with the financial outlook now rosy and the federal budget running a surplus, tax cuts were an easy sell. Coolidge even began to worry that Congress had cut taxes too much and that deficits would return. He warned lawmakers that after the easy work of cutting taxes, they would also have to rein in spending—threatening to veto various appropriations bills if they defied him.[5]

In the end, only a handful of Democrats and progressive Repub-licans voted against the revenue bill. Coolidge signed it at the White House on February 26, 1926, with Mellon beside him, beaming. This was a victory to savor. Economic growth continued to yield tax receipts greater than expected, allowing key appropria-tions bills to pass without busting Coolidge's budget. By July, the president sounded unconcerned about the spending. "The principal thing that will affect the country is the reduction of taxation," he told reporters. "I wasn't able to do a great lot with the reduction of expenditures, but we did keep expenditures down pretty well."[6]

Heading into the fall midterm elections, Coolidge made pros-perity the central issue. Although the president wasn't on the ballot, the GOP hoped to render "support of the administration," as Yale history professor and political commentator William MacDonald put it, "an issue inseparable from that of prosperity." Coolidge's rhetoric highlighted the good times. A ballyhooed preelection address to the Association of American Advertising Agencies was itself an advertisement for his economic stewardship. Speaking to the admen on October 27, the president argued that manufacturers had brought the good life to ever more citizens because of mass production, which relied on mass consumption, which in turn was "created almost entirely through the development of advertising." A classic Coolidge effort to harmonize his faith in old-fashioned industry and his wonder at the consumer economy, the president's talk argued that advertising had a moral as well as an economic purpose. By "minister[ing] to the spiritual side of trade," he said, the craft could ensure that competition didn't "degenerate into a mere selfish scramble for rewards."[7]

If Coolidge's remarks sounded like palaver from Bruce Barton, it was no coincidence. The publicity master had arranged for Coolidge to speak—a favor for Roy Durstine, Barton's partner at the advertising firm and the head of the advertisers' trade group at the time— and also helped to write the president's remarks. Indeed, Barton had become a frequent presidential companion, joining Coolidge most recently at the end of his ten-week summer vacation in the Adirondacks. Barton had suggested he conduct an exclusive interview with the president, contending that it would allow Coolidge to show the world a "human, friendly picture" of himself. The president agreed, his aide Ted Clark explained to Barton, because "your name carried a conviction of sincerity which was absolutely essential."[8]

The interview, reprinted in full by many papers, was anything but sincere. Barton provided Coolidge with the questions beforehand along with proposed answers, and the president drafted replies, which Barton then stitched together. "It was put out . . . in such a way as to be mostly Barton and little of myself," Coolidge later noted. The questions were softballs. Coolidge professed to take great pleasure in doing odds and ends on his Plymouth farm, where he could "repair the fence where it is breaking down, and

mend the latch on the kitchen door"—noting that since most
Americans performed such chores themselves, it helped him "keep
in mind how people live and what is necessary for them to do to get
along." He touched other bases as well: he spoke lovingly of his
wife; he insisted on the need for young boys raised in comfort to
work hard; he praised the press corps as "active, industrious, and
accurate"; and he reminded the country in nonthreatening tones of
his religious faith. "It would be difficult for me to conceive of anyone being able to administer the duties of a great office like the
presidency without a belief in the guidance of a divine providence,"
he declaimed.[9]

The interview was a smash. To be sure, some editorialists derided
the "creamy blandness" of the president's remarks or mocked the
exchange as a stunt, and Delaware senator Thomas F. Bayard, a
Democrat, assailed it as "a press agent effort to sell the president
personally to the country." Yet as Coolidge's confidant Frank Stearns
noted, "Of course some people will bark [but] that merely means
that they are bitten." Critics and admirers alike agreed that the
interview marked, as one critic wrote, a "high tide in publicity . . .
worth to Republican candidates far more than any direct campaign
appeals" by the president in the following weeks.[10]

The Republicans were seeking to equate the president with
prosperity and make the fall vote hinge, as it had in 1924, on
Coolidge's popularity. They ran ads equating the president with
their party—"Do You Believe in Calvin Coolidge Your President?"
asked one; "If You Do, You Have No Alternative But to Vote the
Republican Ticket." But Coolidge's personal appeal turned out not
to be transferable, and the GOP failed to break the normal pattern
for off-year elections, in which the party in the White House suffers
setbacks in Congress. The Republicans lost six seats in the Senate,
including William Butler's, and nine in the House. The defeat
revealed the downside of the new mode of presidential leadership:
by elevating personality over party, it diminished the likelihood of a
president being able to win himself a compliant Congress.[11]

• • •

Apart from taxation, Coolidge also made strides in his second term in minimizing the regulation of business and finance. In his fourth annual message to Congress, on December 7, 1926, he issued a call "for reducing, rather than expanding, government bureaus which seek to regulate and control the business activities of the people." To the objection that workers, consumers, and other citizens needed safeguards, the president replied, "Unfortunately, human nature cannot be changed by an act of the legislature. . . . It is too much assumed that because an abuse exists it is the business of the national government to remedy it."[12]

In one important area, however, Coolidge endorsed new regulation: radio broadcasting. This endorsement represented less a break with his belief in minimal government than an outgrowth of his conviction that government should help a responsible corporate capitalism to thrive. For several years, the absence of federal guidelines had allowed broadcasters' signals that aired on similar frequencies to interfere with one another, ruining the experience of listeners. As a result, broadcasters actually lobbied the government to take a role in supervising their industry. "This important public function has drifted into such chaos," Coolidge acknowledged, "as seems likely, if not remedied, to destroy its great value." Deferring to Commerce Secretary Herbert Hoover, who since the early 1920s had led the way in shaping the expanding medium, Coolidge advised that an ad hoc radio board be created under the aegis of Hoover's department.[13]

The groundbreaking Radio Act that Coolidge signed in February 1927 declared the airwaves public property and therefore subject to government control. It established a five-person panel, the Federal Radio Commission (later the Federal Communications Commission), within the Commerce Department, to issue broadcast licenses and assign frequencies. But the commission would mainly serve the needs of commercial broadcasting. Reflecting Coolidge's belief in a general public interest that trumped the "special" interests of minority groups, the body adopted policies that favored the major broadcasting networks, NBC and CBS. Those networks alone had the ability to provide, as the commission demanded, "a well-rounded program" that included classical and popular music, religion, education, public affairs, news, and weather, and one in which "matters of interest to all members of the family find a place." Stations run by religious groups or universities, which had little hope of furnishing such an array of programming, consistently received poorer treatment. In 1926, noncommercial stations held 28 percent of broadcast licenses; by 1929, they held just 8.6 percent.[14]

"To the man in the street," the *Washington Post* wrote, the Radio Act was "the most important legislation of the session," affecting citizens' daily experiences and those of future radio listeners. While hailed for "clearing the air" of interference, it also served to bolster the power of the emerging giants of broadcasting. It was not so much a victory for pure laissez-faire practice as for the Hamiltonian vision of an ordered society in which government helped large business interests to accrue power in the expectation that they would serve society as a whole.[15]

•   •   •

Coolidge's belief in a minimal federal government was also put to the test when the Mississippi River overflowed its banks in April 1927. Since the previous fall, heavy rains, followed by floods, had wrought havoc in the Midwest. But the president initially turned away entreaties from state governors seeking federal aid. Finally, on April 16, a 1,200-foot stretch of a levee collapsed in southern Illinois; five days later, the force of the torrent broke another levee downriver at Mounds Landing, Mississippi. Hundreds of black laborers working to fortify the riverbanks were swept to oblivion, and it became clear that the waters would cause more death and destruction in the days ahead. Indeed, these floods would culminate in the worst natural disaster in American history until Hurricane Katrina hit New Orleans and the Gulf Coast in 2005.

In the face of this calamity, Coolidge moved swiftly. He convened a cabinet meeting on April 22 and appointed Hoover to lead a federal rescue, relief, and reconstruction effort. Although tensions between the president and his commerce secretary had increased in the second term, Hoover, with his background in relief and his fondness for organization, was an obvious choice for the job. His task, however, would be a huge one, since the disaster had killed hundreds, displaced hundreds of thousands, and produced damages totaling in the hundreds of millions of dollars.

Having delegated the job, Coolidge considered his own duties largely discharged. During the next weeks, entreaties rolled in from governors, senators, and mayors in the afflicted regions, asking him to visit the flood zone. "Your coming would center eyes of nation and the consequent publicity would result in securing millions of dollars additional aid for sufferers," the governor of Mississippi wired. But Coolidge demurred. He likewise declined requests from NBC to broadcast a nationwide appeal and from Will Rogers for a telegram that the humorist might read at an upcoming benefit. The president didn't think he was being callous. He was simply follow-ing his small-government philosophy and sense of thrift. Putting himself at the center of the flood-fighting effort, Coolidge feared, would feed popular demands for a greater federal role in dealing with the disaster—and future ones. Such a change would set a dan-gerous precedent and doom his program of economy.[16]

The private funds Hoover secured for relief and rebuilding, how-ever, were insufficient to the enormous task, and a public debate ensued over whether the federal government should furnish direct aid. Washington had never taken much responsibility for natural disasters. Four decades earlier Grover Cleveland had vetoed a relief bill for Texas drought victims, and even Theodore Roosevelt had demanded local New Orleans banks underwrite federal funds being spent to fight yellow fever there. Coolidge was not the man to break this precedent.[17]

In trying to limit Washington's role, Coolidge had support. "Fortunately, there are still some things that can be done," the *New York Times* declared, "without the wisdom of Congress and the all-fathering federal government." Editorial opinion in the distressed areas, in contrast, was withering. "It has been necessary," wrote the *Jackson Clarion-Ledger,* "to school President Coolidge day by day a bit more towards the realization of the immensity of the catastrophe." Urging the president to use the budget surplus for relief, the *Paducah News-Democrat* concluded that Coolidge had either "the coldest heart in America or the dullest imagination, and we are about ready to believe he has both."[18]

Unremitting coverage of the suffering and damage wrought by the flood increased the pressure on the president. By late spring, however, Congress had adjourned for the year, and a special session would be required to pass any emergency appropriations bill; otherwise such aid would have to wait until the new Congress convened in December. With the floodwaters having subsided, taking care of the displaced, rebuilding the region, and preventing future catastrophes became the order of the day. But Coolidge rejected pleas to convene Congress, and it remained adjourned through the summer and into fall.

Lawmakers from the afflicted regions still pressed for federal help. In late 1927, Illinois's Frank Reid, the Republican chair of the House Flood Control Committee, ratcheted up the pressure by holding public hearings. The move forced the president's hand. In his December 1927 message to Congress, Coolidge endorsed federal flood-control measures, albeit with the key condition that local governments and property owners bear most of the costs. The plan Coolidge backed would cost $296 million, but the Senate and the House—led by lawmakers from the flood regions—put forward plans that would cost considerably more. Another donnybrook between the president and Congress followed.

In February, Coolidge conceded partially on the issue of local contributions. To avoid assuming too large a permanent role for Washington, he specified that only areas flooded in 1927 could depend on more federal aid and less local aid. But even this concession made Coolidge worry about where the funds would go, and when Congress ignored his input he grew intransigent. "President

Coolidge has never shown as much opposition to a measure pending in Congress as he has to this," noted the *New York Times*. It was no exaggeration; in April the president told an aide that he considered the emerging bill "the most radical and dangerous bill that has had the countenance of the Congress since I have been president."[19]

Coolidge had his reasons. As he told reporters on April 10, he feared that Congress had "lost sight of" the goal of protecting those threatened by floods. "It has become a scramble to take care of the railroads and the banks and the individuals who may have invested in levee bonds, and the great lumber concerns that own many thousands of acres in that locality, with wonderful prospects for the contractors." He feared that the appropriation was being larded up with giveaways and that southern corruption would prevent the funds from reaching their intended beneficiaries. Meanwhile, discontent was growing in the distressed areas, leading Will Rogers to remark that Coolidge was going to postpone relief legislation some more in "the hope that those needing relief will perhaps have conveniently died in the meantime."[20]

As the House and Senate struggled in early May to reconcile their versions of the relief bill, Coolidge finally gathered congressional leaders to forge a compromise. A deal was struck: federal financial responsibility would be limited to the areas flooded in 1927 but no contributions were mandated from localities. Deeming the bill "the best that can be obtained from Congress," Coolidge accepted it. Citizens from Cairo to New Orleans celebrated the historic achievement. But Coolidge didn't want to take credit or publicize his support. Declining to host a ceremony, he signed the measure in private on May 15 after finishing his lunch.[21]

• • •

Coolidge responded tepidly to the flood-control bill in part because he never liked to assume huge new federal burdens. But he also knew that his presidency was winding down. For the last nine months he had been, by an act of his own choosing, a lame duck.

After the whirlwind Lindbergh visit in mid-June 1927, Coolidge had gone to the Black Hills to set up his summer White House. He did not go alone. As the *New Republic*'s T.R.B. observed, "No president ever left Washington so elaborately equipped for propaganda purposes. . . . With him [were] some thirty-odd newspaper correspondents, a group of a dozen or more moving-picture men, several unofficial but effective press agents disguised as syndicate writers, a number of expert telegraph operators, camera men representing the photo syndicates . . . a noble company, indeed, and every last man of them devoted to the task of publicity for Mr. Coolidge during the summer months." Throughout the summer, the president continued his twice-weekly press conferences, hosting them from his makeshift office in a room at a Rapid City high school.[22]

The president allowed himself to relax to an unusual degree. He spent many hours in the nearby rivers, stoically hooking worms despite the cavils of the local fishermen, who used flies instead. He took to wearing a cowboy hat, prompting, the Associated Press reported, "a run on the local haberdasheries. . . . Practically the entire secret service corps is fully equipped from books to broad brims, and no small portion of the newspaper crew . . . has succumbed to the dress." On July 4, his fifty-fifth birthday, Coolidge again gratified the cameramen—and made friends and aides wince—by donning a full-scale cowboy outfit, including chaps, silver spurs, a flaming red shirt, blue bandanna, and high-heeled boots. To the delight of a large throng, Coolidge trilled along as a cowboy band played "The Star-Spangled Banner," and the president received as a gift a mare named Kit. The president, who normally looked as if he'd been born in a business suit, would later in the summer don an Indian headdress for the cameras as he spoke to a crowd of ten thousand Sioux as their "Leading Eagle." All the posing suggested to some observers that Coolidge was readying himself for his reelection campaign in 1928.[23]

The news of the summer, however, came on August 2, 1927, four years to the day after Coolidge assumed the presidency. Several days before, he had summoned his secretary, Everett Sanders, to his office in the high school, told him to sit down, and revealed that he wouldn't be seeking another term. "If I should serve as president again," he said, "I should serve almost ten years, which is too long for a president in this country."

"I think the people will be disappointed," Sanders said.

Coolidge gave Sanders a paper with the single sentence, "I do not choose to run for president in 1928," and asked, "What do you think of that?" Concluding that Coolidge "had not the slightest idea of heeding my advice about that unless I should agree," Sanders endorsed the president's decision. They agreed to make the announcement at Coolidge's 9 A.M. press conference on Tuesday the second.[24]

That morning, Coolidge and Sanders discussed their plans. The secretary suggested that it might make sense to wait until midday; given the time difference between Rapid City and New York, he said, the stock market would be closed when the news hit, and traders, having time to digest it, would be less likely to overreact. Coolidge agreed, and he ended his morning parley with reporters by asking them to come back at noon.[25]

At 11:30, the president wrote out the same short sentence on a new sheet of paper and told Sanders to have the stenographer make multiple copies, "five or six on a sheet," and return them to the president. After receiving the sheaf, Coolidge picked up a pair of scissors and meticulously cut the papers into strips. "I am going to hand these out myself. I am going to give them to the newspapermen, without comment, from the side of the desk."[26]

At the appointed hour, the reporters gathered. Quietly delighting as he toyed with them, Coolidge told them to form a line and gave each man a slip. In silence, fittingly, Coolidge had announced the end of his presidency as suddenly as he had begun it.

The reporters were flummoxed. They begged the president for more information. But Coolidge, with his characteristic passive aggression, just savored their confusion. "There will be nothing more from this office today," he needled them with a smile. He turned to Kansas senator Arthur Capper, who was visiting, and suggested they head off to have lunch and then to fish.[27]

In the car, Capper fished for an explanation. "Well, that was a sudden announcement you made this morning, Mr. President. It took them by surprise."

"It's four years ago today since I became president," Coolidge replied. "If I take another term, I will be in the White House till 1933. . . . Ten years in Washington is longer than any other man has had it—too long!" It is not quite accurate to say Coolidge was concerned that another term would somehow violate the custom of serving only two terms, for he had been elected only to one. But the assumption underlying that custom—that presidents shouldn't become too powerful—was clearly at work.[28]

When the men arrived at the summer White House, Grace Coolidge joined them for lunch. Avoiding his bombshell, the president talked eagerly about a visit from local Indian leaders, then promptly retired for his nap. Capper, left alone with the first lady, asked her about Coolidge's noontime announcement.

"What announcement?" she replied.[29]

Coolidge's news gave rise to endless conjecture. Why did he word the statement as he had? Why "choose to run"? Was he leaving the door open for a draft? There is little evidence that he harbored such hopes, and in his autobiography he said that he never decided what to do if he were drafted, because "I was determined not to have that contingency arise." Nor is there much basis for the claim that he foresaw a financial downturn. Rather, the statements Coolidge made to Sanders and Capper are consistent with what he told Edmund Starling that spring. "The novelty of being president had worn off," the agent recalled Coolidge saying. "The glory of it had gone with Calvin's death; there was no great national crisis which demanded a continuation of his leadership. From now on, the office was more of a burden than anything else." In his autobiography, Coolidge said he "had a desire to be relieved of the pretensions and delusions of public life."[30]

For all the parsing Coolidge's brief statement received, his decision no longer seems like such a mystery. Besides the reasons he gave, he simply never relished power or the office the way other presidents did, and he had no great unfinished agenda. His moral sense enabled him to apply to himself the same strictures against power in the executive that he wished to place on others. "The chances of having wise and faithful public service are increased by a change in the presidential office after a moderate length of time," he wrote, expressing a sentiment that, if a tad sanctimonious, was surely sincerely felt. Finally, there was his health and that of his wife. Neither was seriously ill, but Grace was wearying of her duties and Calvin had always been a bit of a hypochondriac.[31]

The remaining year and a half of Coolidge's presidency would not lack for activity or achievements: Morrow's Mexican diplomacy in late 1927, Coolidge's Havana speech in 1928, the flood-control bill that spring, the Kellogg-Briand pact in August, and Jose Moncada's election in Nicaragua in November—as well as a final round of Mellon tax cuts to crown Coolidge's presidency. There would be fights over farm relief in the form of the McNary-Haugen bill and the familiar quadrennial speculation over who would be the next president. (Coolidge's judgment: "They're going to elect that superman Hoover, and he's going to have some trouble.") Then, too, the soaring stock market would in December 1927 begin the stratospheric climb that would thrill the nation—and continue skyward through and beyond Calvin Coolidge's last year in office.[32]

10

———

A Contested Legacy

With Grace at his side, Calvin Coolidge rode to Union Station on the afternoon of March 4, 1929, under a dull gray Washington drizzle. For days the president had watched the preparation for Herbert Hoover's inaugural festivities as if it were, in the words of White House usher Ike Hoover (no relation), "the building of a scaffold for his execution." On Inauguration Day itself, Coolidge walked dutifully beside his successor in the ritual parade, then watched the swearing-in in the Senate chambers. By the afternoon, Coolidge was president no more. He and Grace boarded a Pullman car and headed back to New England—immensely admired, credited with having nourished good times, and even, in the eyes of some, revered for having midwifed the bounteous New Era.[1]

The press deemed Coolidge's presidency a success. Although some signs of looming danger had emerged in 1928, they were too few, too dim, and too easily eclipsed by the neon-bright shine of the stock market boom for the president or most other Americans to take heed. Few quarreled with the judgment that Coolidge had made in his final State of the Union message in December 1928. "No Congress of the United States ever assembled, on surveying the state of the Union, has met with a more pleasing prospect than that which appears at the present time," he said. "In the domestic field there is tranquility and contentment . . . and the highest record of years of prosperity. In the foreign field there is peace, the goodwill which comes from mutual understanding."[2]

Critics derided still Coolidge's deference to business, his lack of ambition, and his passivity. Walter Lippmann mocked the president's "genius for inactivity": "Nobody has ever worked harder at inactivity, with such force of character, with such unremitting attention to detail, with such conscientious devotion to the task," the influential columnist wrote. But a satisfied majority didn't complain. Just as Coolidge's asceticism and rectitude commended him to a public warily entering a new culture, so his reluctance to embark on visionary programs seemed to bespeak a healthy moderation. "People turned with relief and confidence" after the Progressive Era and the war, explained Bruce Bliven of the *New Republic*, "toward a man who clearly would never in his life do anything rash." "While I don't expect anything very astonishing from him," added Supreme Court justice Oliver Wendell Holmes, "I don't want anything very astonishing."[3]

· · ·

Before Coolidge left office, he would enjoy a final year of "Coolidge Prosperity." His last year as president, 1928, seemed to be the capstone atop a six-year run of growth—with the profits on Wall Street climbing so high and so fast that some now talked of the "Coolidge Market" as well. But beneath the good times, structural weaknesses lurked in the American economy, and even as the stock market soared, those underlying problems remained unsolved.

The first problem was that, late in Coolidge's term, as investment was overheating into speculation, business activity was actually cooling. The housing market had begun to soften in 1926, sales of cars, appliances, and other durable goods flagged in 1927, and construction leveled off in 1928. The saturation of these industries boded ill, for the economy had become unduly reliant on sales of houses and cars. These sectors were the props of a house of cards, and their inability to bear more weight meant that when they collapsed, so would the whole economy.[4]

Inequality compounded the difficulty. Although Coolidge Prosperity had enriched many, wealth remained unevenly distributed. From 1923 to 1929, the share of income reaped by the topmost tier of Americans grew. Although business profits mounted, consumers saw little of the gains. According to a 1928 Brookings Institution report, more than half of American families remained near or below a subsistence level. Agriculture, coal, and textile workers suffered acutely. This maldistribution of wealth and income compounded the downturn in key economic sectors, because poorer Americans, including farmers and low-wage workers—many of whom still wanted to buy homes and cars and appliances in the decade's later years—remained barred at the gates of the new economy. Unable to join in the consumption, they were also powerless to reinvigorate these tapped-out industries.[5]

The economic softening of the late 1920s drew little comment. Masking its ill effects was the bull market, which had been charging ahead with only minor setbacks since 1924. Although taken by laymen as a marker of economic strength, the stock market fever actually signaled that productive long-term investment opportunities were drying up. By late 1927, investment was giving way to trading that was clearly speculative, motivated not by the sound study of specific firms and underlying conditions but by the simple wish to turn a fast buck. Many companies, ignoring the rule that equates prudent management with modest payments to shareholders and substantial reinvestment of profits, fed the mania for increased dividends and capital gains. By early 1928 investors were playing the market entirely on expectations of additional increases—the classic definition of a bubble.[6]

Adding to the frenzy, stock trading, once the preserve of the wealthy, was now enticing the middle class. Although only perhaps one in a hundred Americans actually bought stocks, this percentage still meant that hordes of new investors were flooding the brokerage houses setting up shop across the country. Millions more followed the ticker tape as keenly as the major league box scores. Noninvestors made judgments about their futures based on the financial indices' upward course, tying their fates to those of the rich, while those who did invest traded feverishly. In the first week of December 1927, more stock shares were bought and sold than in any other week in the annals of the New York exchange. New benchmarks were set the following March, June, and November. In 1928 some 1.1 billion shares were exchanged—an almost fivefold increase over 1923.

In March 1928, as Coolidge's final year as president opened, the market paused for what seemed to be an imminent correction but then began to soar again. Led by radio and automobile stocks—the success stories of the 1920s—indices climbed skyward. On some days or weeks, gains defied imagination. Any pauses and slides, meanwhile—even big ones—soon gave way to new spikes.

A few Cassandras warned that what goes up must come down. William Z. Ripley, a Harvard economist, visited the White House in 1926 to point out that the growing number of stockholders in the market had little control over corporate decisions affecting their fates, but he concluded—to Coolidge's relief—that the federal government could do nothing about it. In addition, several far-sighted journalists and economists fretted about the potential fallout from the decade's widening inequality. The popular economists William Foster and Waddill Catchings published *Business Without a Buyer* (1927) and *The Road to Plenty* (1928), books that dissented from the gospel of productivity. Casting doubt on Say's Law and the idea that supply created its own demand, the authors prescribed a proto-Keynesianism, arguing that the government should superintend the provision of adequate consumer income, especially when business production softened.

These and other doomsayers, of course, turned out to be generally correct—if not in all of their particulars—and in retrospect it's easy to chide Americans for ignoring the red flags. It's easy, too, to fault them for not learning from the decade's previous orgies of glorified gambling—Charles Ponzi's 1920 pyramid swindle or the fraud-ridden Florida real estate boom that finally ebbed in 1925 and 1926—in which get-rich-quick promises proved too good to be true. But if Foster and Catchings reached a popular audience with their tracts, even wider readerships were claimed by books and articles with titles like *New Levels in the Stock Market,* in which prophets of the New Era argued that a revolution in industry, trade, and finance had tamed the dreaded business cycle and that Wall Street's climb need not end. These optimists foresaw a cornucopian future in which consumer spending would provide an ever-rising standard of living. The productivity of the age was obvious and undeniable; the dangerous maldistribution of its benefits was more easily tolerated or ignored.[7]

The market's ascent clouded the thinking of politicians as well. Herbert Hoover accepted his party's nomination to succeed Coolidge in 1928 by heralding the end of indigence. "We in America are nearer today to the final triumph over poverty than ever before in the history of any land," he declared. "The poorhouse is vanishing from among us." More laconic, but as complacent, was Andrew Mellon. "There is no cause for worry," the Treasury secretary declared. "The high tide of prosperity will continue." Most Democrats, for their part, either shared the euphoria or feared mounting an assault on the popular Coolidge. They chose as their national committee chairman John Raskob, a General Motors executive who listed his occupation in *Who's Who* as "capitalist," wooed big business, and wrote a magazine article entitled "Everybody Ought to Be Rich," which mapped a path to affluence for anyone game enough to play the market.[8]

For months, the market seemed to justify these hopes. In the fall of 1928, new pinnacles dwarfed those of the spring. After Coolidge passed the reins of power to Hoover in March 1929, share prices climbed still higher. That every drop was followed by a rebound assuaged many skeptics. Stories circulated of the broker's valet who made $250,000, of the nurse who turned patients' tips into $30,000, of the peddler who parlayed his $4,000 savings into sixty times that amount. The veracity of these tales was beside the point.[9]

The collapse began in September. Leading stocks starting losing value, some as much as 30 percent. Yet investors, having learned that dips provided opportunities to buy low, stood firm. This time, though, the slide continued. On October 24, Black Thursday, investors unloaded stocks en masse. After the market appeared to stabilize on Friday, the plunge continued with the start of trading the next week. The decline persisted for a fortnight, until on November 13 the market hit a low for the year. Industrial stocks had lost half their value. Some $100 billion in assets had vanished.

What made the crash truly horrific was the Depression that followed. Though economists generally believe that the crash didn't directly cause the Depression, the events of late October and November 1929 clearly kneecapped the economy. Banks grew wary of lending and called in loans; over the next four years, nine thousand institutions would shutter their doors, draining the economy of money. Sapped of their confidence, corporations—which even before the crash had slowed the pace of new investment—tightened their belts further, shedding employees, lopping inventories, and deferring new spending. Cash-strapped consumers bought less, depleting the economy of ready money. There followed a prolonged period of unemployment, stagnant production, and privation that shattered millions of lives. So severe was the crisis that one-quarter to one-third of the labor force would be out of work by 1933. It would take until 1937 for production to regain its 1929 levels.

• • •

What was Coolidge's role in this terrible shift from boom to bust? Standard accounts affix some blame to his policies. His laxity toward regulating business, on this view, led him to ignore calls for changes in the financial industry and to tolerate stock market speculation. His fiscal and monetary policies fueled the recklessness; he appeared to believe that benefits would trickle down to the masses in substantial volume, no matter what the distribution of income, wealth, economic power, or profitable investment opportunities.

Meanwhile, his bungling of international trade and credit issues allowed the time bomb of European currency instability and competitive devaluation to tick on. "The administration took the narrow interest of business groups to be the national interest," the historian William Leuchtenburg wrote, "and the result was catastrophe."[10]

Others, however, shield Coolidge from personal responsibility, emphasizing the general popularity of his policies. Few people, after all, imagined that the props beneath the entire stock market were so frail; fewer still imagined that the bust that followed the boom would last so long or cut so deep. On this view, Coolidge stands guilty only of lacking clairvoyance—or at worst of sharing a too-high estimation of the cooperative spirit of American corporations. Even Coolidge's harshest critics agree that the roots of the Depression lie deeper than any policies of one man. In *The Great Crash, 1929*, John Kenneth Galbraith wrote that to assail Coolidge for his "superficial optimism" about the economy, as so many historians have done, is "grossly unfair." Coolidge was hardly outside the mainstream thought of his day.[11]

A series of Coolidge's economic policies can thus be examined, with an eye not toward condemnation or exoneration—a fool's game—but toward understanding the dominant thinking of his day. First, what is most plainly apparent in retrospect is that the stock market needed more regulation but the general prosperity of the 1920s, combined with Coolidge's own predilections and the absence of precedent for such intervention, kept the president from imposing the needed controls. As a result, unwitting investors were left vulnerable to stockjobbers' schemes to drive up prices—such as selling shares back and forth to one another to create the false impression of strong interest in a stock. After the crash, a congressional investigation exposed some of these secretive, self-serving practices, but such findings offered cold comfort to those who had lost their livelihoods.[12]

Moreover, while some of Wall Street's unsavory practices were hatched behind closed doors, the most significant one occurred in full public view. Margin trading—buying stocks with a pittance of a down payment and a loan from one's broker, then selling them at a profit soon thereafter—became a favorite ticket to riches. Like Ponzi's scheme, it depended on the buyer not getting caught short when the bill came due. Here, some market watchers sounded warnings, urging the Federal Reserve banks to stop the loans to brokers that facilitated these deals. But Coolidge tolerated the banks' loose lending. In January 1928, when brokers' loans had reached a volume of $3.8 billion—$1 billion more than just a year before— a reporter asked the president if they had gotten out of control. Coolidge said no. The surge, he maintained, reflected the growing volume of bank deposits accruing and of new stocks being issued. The president's comment surprised financiers and drew angry criticism. In the Senate, Robert La Follette Jr., carrying the Progressive flame for his late father, introduced a resolution calling on the Fed to restrain its banks, but he had no success.[13]

Beyond the regulation of Wall Street, there was the second and broader issue of the money supply. Then as now, presidents were not supposed to second-guess (much less influence) the Federal Reserve, and Coolidge raised no objections to the agency's loose-money program. Unfortunately, the Fed pursued an unwise course. In 1927, as speculation was growing, it deferred to the wishes of European finance ministers and actually cut interest rates in the hope of inflating prices and equalizing trade imbalances. Then, when it did move to control trading, it was too tentative. Starting in January 1928, the Fed began to raise the discount rate, from 3.5 to 5 percent, in the hope of discouraging loans, and in February 1929, the board, weighing in on the brokers' loans controversy, urged its own banks to "restrain the use . . . of Federal Reserve facilities in aid of the growth of speculative credit." In response to these mild steps, the market stalled briefly—but then resumed its climb. A more forceful campaign against the speculative loans, including words from the president, might have helped check the practice, but neither the Fed nor Coolidge—already eyeing retirement—saw fit to intervene.[14]

Third, Coolidge promulgated a fiscal policy that encouraged speculation and ignored inequality. Coolidge's tax cuts had given investors more dollars to feed the market, helping to push the healthy investment of the mid-1920s into the gambling that followed. A flat tax on capital gains encouraged investors to buy the rapidly appreciating stocks instead of bonds. And because corporations (thanks to lower taxes overall) were showing higher profits, they became more alluring to investors—an allure that in retrospect they clearly didn't deserve. Finally, these fiscal policies exacerbated the uneven distribution of buying power that made the Depression so severe.

Fourth, addressing the problem of inequality would have meant taking on the farm crisis. As a group, farmers shared little in the prosperity of the 1920s, but Coolidge never saw eye to eye with the farm bloc on how to help their debt-strapped constituents. Many progressives embraced a panacea known as McNary-Haugenism—a proposal dating to 1921 that was taken up in 1924 by Senator Charles McNary of Oregon and Representative Gilbert Haugen of Iowa. The McNary-Haugen bill promised to relieve farmers by creating a federal board that would buy crop surpluses at a price that reflected the higher prewar ratio of farm prices to the general price index; it would then dump the crops on the world market at a loss or on the domestic market when prices had rebounded. After much struggle, a version passed Congress in 1926. But Coolidge vetoed it in 1927 and vetoed a second version in 1928. His reasons were many. The scheme would have encouraged farmers to grow more crop than the market would bear; its dumping provisions posed dangers for the international economy; it would have raised prices for consumers; and, to the president's mind, it smacked of government management of markets and favored a minority group over the common good. But if Coolidge was correct to kill the bill, the reforms he proposed instead were insubstantial, and the hard times for farmers dragged on—with repercussions for the entire American economy.

A fifth factor that contributed to the Depression was the imbalance in global trade and credit, which wiser tariff and currency policies might have helped remedy. This problem began with the European debt issues that the Dawes Plan was supposed to have solved. But despite some short-term improvements in the European economies in the middle of the decade, in 1928 Germany was still crippled by its reparations, and the Allies still owed large sums to the United States. Lower tariffs would have helped European nations sell their goods in the United States, but Coolidge supported high imposts as a means to help American business. The result was bad news all around—a burden on foreign economies, a risk for American banks, and, as it turned out, a recipe for trade-wrecking international retaliation.

Finally, the demise of the gold standard in international trade contributed to the global financial problem. By the 1920s, many European nations had abandoned the gold standard, allowing their currencies to float in value. But the United States had not; American creditors still insisted on being paid in dollars or gold. This discrepancy led debtor nations to pay up in gold, creating an influx of gold bullion into the United States—an accumulation that fueled the explosion of credit that underlay the feverish American speculation of the last years of the decade.

All these policies played some part in bringing about the economic crisis of the 1930s. To what degree American economic policy, conducted differently, could have produced a different outcome is unknowable, and any president surely would have failed to do all that was necessary to avert some serious trouble. But Coolidge's naive faith in the gospel of productivity and the benevolence of business—as well as his excessive reliance on others to make his policies—deterred him even from asking the questions that might have mitigated the misfortune. His robust popularity confirmed the reality of the prosperity that bore his name, and the prosperity confirmed for him the wisdom of his philosophy. As he set off for Northampton in March 1929, he had no inkling of the disasters that loomed just seven months off.

• • •

As Coolidge began his retirement years in Northampton, he remained an object of popular affection. Well-wishers and hand-shakers greeted him everywhere. Reporters peered in his car window; one tried to enter his bathroom while he was showering. Tourists paraded by the duplex home on Massasoit Street to which he had returned. Coolidge didn't like the attention, and in 1930 he bought a large house on the outskirts of town called The Beeches.

It was an uncharacteristic indulgence; for the most part Coolidge lived simply. Friends and colleagues from Frank Stearns to Edmund Starling came to visit, but the former president returned to Washington only once, at Hoover's invitation, to celebrate the signing of the Kellogg-Briand Treaty in July 1929—and at the day's end he took the night train home. He traveled little. "I get so much newspaper reaction if I go anywhere that the only place I am safe is at home," he explained to his former secretary Ted Clark. Coolidge took just one major trip in his post-presidential years, to Florida, New Orleans, and the West. In California Will Hays arranged a tour of the movie studios and William Randolph Hearst hosted the former president at his San Simeon castle.[15]

Coolidge also stayed out of politics. "I am trying," he wrote to Chief Justice Taft, "to avoid making speeches or attending public gatherings." He abstained from Republican Party affairs and sought no platform as an elder statesman. Some of his friends, including Harlan Fiske Stone, had encouraged him to run for the Senate, but Coolidge believed it wouldn't be proper for a former president to do so. He spurned offers to cash in on his celebrity by promoting products, such as his trademark cigars. "Whatever influence I might have came to me because of the position I have held, and to use that influence in any competitive field would be unfair. . . . These people are trying to hire not Calvin Coolidge but a former president of the United States." Albert Lasker, the advertising mogul and Republican public relations adviser, offered $75,000 to use Grace Coolidge's name in a promotional contest, but the former president declined on her behalf.[16]

Coolidge's withdrawal wasn't absolute. He took on a few ceremonial duties, such as serving on a national committee to study
transportation problems. He assumed the honorary leadership of
the Harding Memorial Association and the presidency of the American Antiquarian Society—though with his long-standing amateur
interest in the American past, the latter was more a labor of love
than of public service. For work, he accepted a relatively uncontro-
versial position with New York Life Insurance. Apart from the occasional trip to New York City for that job, he worked out of the same
office in Northampton he had used years before.

To the extent that Coolidge remained a public presence, it was
largely as a writer. His autobiography, published in late 1929, just
after the crash, brought him a large advance. Although trumpeted
in newspaper ads as "The greatest American autobiography since
BEN FRANKLIN," the book provoked some harsh reviews. Spare in
style and superficial in analysis, brightened by only a few flashes of
wit and emotion, it was notable mainly for certifying Coolidge's
aversion to self-disclosure. It scarcely dealt with policy issues and
dished precious little gossip.[17]

The following July, in a cushy deal with his friend Hearst, the
former president began writing a daily syndicated column with the
resolutely unpretentious title "Calvin Coolidge Says" (in some papers
titled "Thinking Things Over with Calvin Coolidge"). The column
offered plainspoken, tepid, and bromidic commentary on public
affairs. Roughly a hundred newspapers carried the column, paying
record sums for it, and it earned the president close to $200,000
(more than $2 million in 2006 dollars)—and drew the kind of
rebukes for trading on his service that he otherwise scrupulously
avoided. In any event, Coolidge found the writing taxing and quit
after a year.

The Depression furthered Coolidge's withdrawal from public
life. Hoover, headstrong and self-confident, didn't seek his predecessor's advice. The snub irritated Coolidge. As Grace later con-
fided, he lacked confidence in Hoover's leadership, in the manner
that "all former presidents think the country is going to the dogs

when another man 'takes over.' " But Coolidge was hard-pressed to offer any bright ideas of his own. He struggled to understand how his wise policies were now scorned as myopic or injurious. In his newspaper column, he maintained in his naive way that optimism and pluck could vanquish the hard times.[18] He sometimes rose to defend his administration's economic policies, which were now coming under fire as the Depression deepened, though he did so without gusto. Privately, he conceded, as Ted Clark told Bruce Barton, that "matters would [not] have been entirely different had he, Coolidge, been in office." Charles Andrews, an Amherst professor and friend of the president's, maintained that Coolidge came to regret his inaction in the face of the stock market bubble.[19]

In fact, noted Andrews, the president was gloomier about the chances of a recovery than his public pronouncements suggested. "In other periods of depression," Coolidge told the professor, "it has always been possible to see some things which were solid and upon which you could base hope, but as I look back I see nothing to give ground for hope, nothing of man. But there is still religion, which is the same as yesterday, today, and forever." The recourse to religion provided Coolidge with an escape from his sadness, as it did for many who suffered. Indeed, a good number of Americans still venerated the former president for his simple piety, and some urged him to run for president in 1932 or 1936.[20]

Yet for all his loyal admirers, Coolidge was coming increasingly to be seen as a relic from a bygone era. The view that he had been derelict in tackling burgeoning problems caught hold. "Nero fiddled, but Coolidge only snored," cracked H. L. Mencken, rehearsing the lore about the president's napping. Many liberals had long assailed Coolidge's economics, but now they claimed vindication. In the *New Republic*, Matthew Josephson mocked the conceits of the New Era, playing back to Coolidge his declaration that the United States "had entered the charmed circle of diminished expenditures, diminishing tax rates, and increasing profits." Coolidge's foreign policy, too, was judged with new harshness for its shortsightedness, while his passive conception of the presidential office was rapidly deemed antiquated. "He tackled few [problems] and settled none of them. Not a word came out of him on the subject of Prohibition," continued Mencken. "Not once did he challenge the speculative lunacy that finally brought the nation to bankruptcy. And all he could be induced to do about the foreign debts was to hand the nuisance on to poor Hoover. . . . That this normalcy was itself full of dangers did not occur to anyone."[21]

By the summer of 1932, just three and half years after leaving office, Coolidge's health began to decline. Only sixty years old, he complained of bronchitis, asthma, and indigestion. He turned down an invitation to open the Olympic Games, held that summer in Los Angeles, citing his physical condition. He refused to stump for Hoover in the fall campaign, apart from delivering one speech in Madison Square Garden in October and a radio talk from The Beeches on election eve—neither of which did anything to forestall Franklin Roosevelt's landslide victory. As 1933 approached, Coolidge's friends received notes in which he bemoaned his listlessness. "I find I am more and more worn out," he wrote to Starling. Ted Clark described him as "very much worried and greatly depressed."[22]

On January 5, Coolidge left his Northampton office in midmorning, telling his secretary he was going home to rest. When Grace Coolidge went up to his room to fetch him for lunch, she found him lying on his back in his dressing area. He had suffered a fatal heart attack.

The outpouring of grief that followed showed that if Coolidge was becoming a token of a lost age, that age still evoked fondness and nostalgia as well as regret. President Hoover ordered thirty days of public mourning. The funeral was held in Northampton two days later on a gray, drizzling Saturday. The pallbearers included Stearns and Butler. From Washington came, among others, the Hoovers, Charles Evans Hughes (now chief justice), Associate Justice Harlan Fiske Stone, Henry Stimson (now secretary of state), and Eleanor Roosevelt—the wife of the president-elect. The ceremony, at the Coolidges' redbrick Congregational church, lasted a mere twenty minutes. A hearse drove the president's coffin to Plymouth Notch, where Coolidge was buried.

The timing of Coolidge's death had a certain poignancy. Marking the end of an era, it occurred just two months before Franklin Delano Roosevelt took office to implement the radical economic changes—Coolidge had privately called them "socialistic"—of the New Deal. In December 1932, just a month after FDR's election, Coolidge himself had conceded that times had changed, perhaps irreversibly. "We are in a new era to which I do not belong," he lamented to a friend, "and it would not be possible for me to adjust to it."[23]

. . .

Like spectators at a Greek tragedy, contemporary readers of Coolidge's story know how the drama will end. They can only watch with anger, anguish, or pity as he ineluctably pursues the policies that seemed so wise then and so foolish later on. For this reason, as well as for personal ones, Coolidge seems today to be at bottom a sad figure.

The loss of family members had early on predisposed Calvin Coolidge toward fatalism and sorrow. Those deep wounds didn't stop him from developing friendships, ambition, or a dry sense of humor. But they reinforced a shyness that would always distance him from others, confining him behind psychological barriers he could never fully surmount. The cruel death of Calvin Jr. etched a permanent scar; adding to his grief, the president's father died in March 1926, just shy of eighty-one—depriving Coolidge's frequent visits to his native Plymouth of their customary comfort. When the former president retreated there in retirement, he was often seen visiting the family plot.

His temperament and heartbreaks aside, the sadness that friends detected when they paid call on Coolidge—less moroseness than melancholy—seems also to have been a grieving for the lost glory of his presidency. For years afterward, Coolidge seemed fixed in time during a naive era of a restrained presidency and an unrestrained

faith in business. Soon Franklin Roosevelt would transform the relationship of the federal government to the economy and of the
White House to policy making. Among myriad other consequences,
the new expectations of the American president—expectations of
activism and far-sighted vision—would make it seem that history
had passed Calvin Coolidge by.

For two generations, the historical shifts of the 1930s and 1940s
made Coolidge a near-triviality. To the contemporary scholar of his
presidency, however, those shifts make rendering any clean verdict
a challenge; it requires a kind of bifocal vision to see his policies
from the vantage of both his own day and ours. After all, to judge
Coolidge only by the standards that his countrymen used is to risk
solipsism—denying a role for the perspective that time and change
can afford. To extol Coolidge because he was popular or because
he presided over real prosperity is not so much wrong as it is
incomplete.

On the other hand, to evaluate Coolidge solely by the standards
of the post–New Deal era is to risk anachronism—holding him
accountable for not being ahead of his time. The dismal rankings
assigned to him by historians in the presidential ratings game seem,
on this view, not so much unfair as irrelevant. Like his fellow base-
ment dwellers Hoover and Harding, Coolidge was a creature of his
times. To fault Coolidge for not knowing the lessons of the Depression and the New Deal is ahistorical and to assume that those lessons represent history's final verdict is dangerous. The recrudescent
conservatism of the late twentieth century has already given new
appeal in some quarters to Coolidge's philosophy—and has
reopened debates about the wisdom of his policies that were once
considered closed.

This, then, is the dilemma of Coolidge—and of the 1920s—as
seen by history. The optimism of the age that overrode anxieties
about the exploding consumer economy; the reassurances Coolidge
gave to a public uncertain about its takeoff into modernity; the dis-
regard for politics and government when business seemed to be
forging a New Era—all these tendencies defined the decade and

gave it its heady rush. It is fair enough to pronounce them, in hind-sight, the tokens of a self-satisfied people and leadership. But latter-day retrospection should not come at the expense of appreciating how people experienced the culture of their day—or what President Coolidge, as a symbol as well as a political actor, meant to his public.

Coolidge has typically been stereotyped as a throwback to the nineteenth century. But that analysis, while accurate in capturing his attachment to the rural values and old-fashioned tastes of his upbringing, isn't fully satisfying. Confining Coolidge to the culture of an earlier America can't account for the ways he ushered the country into the modern age.

Coolidge was the first president whom more than a sliver of the public could see and hear with any frequency—and thus come to feel as if they knew intimately. One survey ranked him first among "the most photographed persons on earth outside of movieland." The image America saw of Coolidge, moreover, was not one prom-ulgated naively, as the president's purposeful reliance on the lead-ing public relations men of his day showed.[24]

The result of this unprecedented exposure for an American president was more than familiarity; it was the foundation of a modern presidential style. "Repeatedly he has utilized this instru-mentality [of radio] to give the people his views simultaneously in all parts of the country," noted Bascom Slemp in 1926. "It may, in part, account for the unanimity of sentiment now prevailing on public issues." Believing in a single, common good, Coolidge con-ceived of himself—by virtue of his office as well as his views—as representative of the public as a whole; deeming members of Con-gress captive to special interests, he sought to lead by going over their heads. Thus, if he fared poorly in the presidential duty to get a program through Congress, he was eminently successful in fulfill-ing the other function of the presidency—to be a representative symbol and visible embodiment of the people. When former sena-tor Chauncey Depew of New York said of Coolidge, "We've got a leader for a president," he was referring not to his legislative achievements but to his symbolic power.[25]

Because of this modern approach to governance—and his faith in the New Era—it is more helpful to see Coolidge as a bridge between two epochs than to label him a vestige of Victorianism. "The world broke in two in 1922 or thereabouts," said the novelist Willa Cather, revising Virginia Woolf's aphorism about human character changing on or about December 1910. The exact date aside—for there is no exact date—America was in transition in these years, and it needed leaders to express its ambivalent disposition. Coolidge deployed twentieth-century methods to promote nineteenth-century values—and used nineteenth-century values to soothe the apprehension caused by twentieth-century dislocations. Straddling the two eras, he spoke for a nation in flux.[26]

Moreover, the ideas Coolidge stood for and the people he spoke for turned out not to be as obsolescent as they later seemed. The liberal consensus of the midcentury years, presumed by many to be permanent, was itself a creature of a particular historical moment, and even as Coolidge was fading from memory, people like Ronald Reagan embraced the ideals he personified. As big government in its time fell into disrepute, much as Coolidge's small government had a generation before, Coolidge's axioms regained favor.

Even upon Coolidge's death, the argument for his rehabilitation was already being made—ironically, by no less than H. L. Mencken, whose nihilism always contained as much conservative scorn for government as liberal disdain for cultural reaction. "We suffer most when the White House busts with ideas," Mencken wrote, citing the failures of Wilson and Hoover. "With a world saver preceding him (I count out Harding as a mere hallucination) and a Wonder Boy following him, [Coolidge] begins to seem, in retrospect, an extremely comfortable and even praiseworthy citizen. . . . If the day ever comes when Jefferson's warnings are heeded at last, and we reduce government to its simplest terms, it may very well happen that Cal's bones now resting inconspicuously in the Vermont granite will come to be revered as those of a man who really did the nation some service." For legions of Americans who did seek a government pared to its simplest terms, Coolidge's virtues and attitudes would return a half century after his passing as inspiration—even if many of the foot soldiers of the New Right had little memory or even historical knowledge of the man himself. As Coolidge's attitudes gained influence again under Reagan and his Republican successors, and Silent Cal's virtues took on a nostalgic glow, these legatees would derive no small sense of triumph—even as their triumph meant that the failings and limitations of Calvin Coolidge's presidency would also have to be discovered anew.[27]

Notes

In this book endnotes will be used not to cite every fact but to attribute quotations, certain statistics, and potentially controversial claims, as well as to elaborate on detail beyond that found in the main text.

INTRODUCTION

1. *New York Times*, January 22, 1981, p. B8.
2. Alice Roosevelt Longworth, *Crowded Hours* (New York: Charles Scribner's Sons, 1933), p. 337; H. L. Mencken, *On Politics: A Carnival of Buncombe* (Baltimore: Johns Hopkins University Press, 1996 [1956]), pp. 123–24; Nathanael West, *A Cool Million*, in *Novels and Other Writings* (New York: Library of America, 1997), pp. 127–238. The line about the pickle is often attributed to Longworth, but she wrote that she heard it from her doctor, who heard it from his previous patient.
3. Ronald Reagan, *An American Life* (New York: Simon & Schuster, 1990), pp. 244, 282; *New York Times*, July 16, 1985, p. A11; Thomas B. Silver, *Coolidge and the Historians* (Durham, NC: Carolina Academic Press for the Claremont Institute, 1982); Kiron Skinner, Annelise Anderson, and Martin Anderson, eds., *Reagan: A Life in Letters* (New York: Free Press, 2003), p. 287. For an excellent discussion of Coolidge's influence on Reagan, see Colleen Shogan, "Coolidge and Reagan: The Rhetorical Influence of Silent Cal on the Great Communicator," *Rhetoric & Public Affairs* 9, no. 2 (Summer 2006), pp. 215–34.
4. Jude Wanniski, *The Way the World Works* (Washington, DC: Regnery, 1998 [1978]), pp. 131–32, passim; Robert Novak, "Coolidge's

Legacy," *New England Journal of History* 55, no.1 (Fall 1998); "Why I Wear What I Wear," *GQ*, June 1988, p. 74.

5. *Washington Post*, June 7, 1981, p. A3. See also Alan Brinkley, "Calvin Reagan," *New York Times*, July 4, 1981, p. A19.

6. Novak, "Coolidge's Legacy," p. 13.

7. Calvin Coolidge, "Our Heritage from Hamilton," address on the anniversary of the birth of Alexander Hamilton, presented at the Hamilton Club, Chicago, January 11, 1922, in *The Price of Freedom: Speeches and Addresses* (New York: Charles Scribner's Sons, 1924), p. 112.

8. Calvin Coolidge, "The Press Under a Free Government," address before the American Society of Newspaper Editors, January 17, 1925, in *Foundations of the Republic: Speeches and Addresses* (New York: Charles Scribner's Sons, 1926), pp. 187, 190.

9. Lynd and Lynd quoted in Nathan Miller, *New World Coming: The 1920s and the Making of Modern America* (New York: Scribner, 2003), p. 172; Edmund Starling, *Starling of the White House* (New York: Simon & Schuster, 1946), p. 243.

10. On Barton, see Jackson Lears, "From Salvation to Self-Realization: Advertising and the Therapeutic Roots of the Consumer Culture, 1880–1930," in *The Culture of Consumption: Critical Essays in American History, 1880–1980*, ed. Richard Wightman Fox and Jackson Lears (New York: Pantheon Books, 1983), p. 31. On Ford, see Steven Watts, *The People's Tycoon: Henry Ford and the American Century* (New York: Alfred A. Knopf, 2005).

11. Fitzgerald quoted in Jay Parini, introduction to F. Scott Fitzgerald, *The Beautiful and the Damned* (New York: Penguin Putnam, 1998), p. ix.

12. Walter Lippmann, *Men of Destiny* (New York: Macmillan, 1927), p. 17.

13. Walter Lippmann, *Liberty and the News* (New York: Harcourt, Brace and Howe, 1920), pp. 55–56; C. Bascom Slemp, *The Mind of the President: As Revealed by Himself in His Own Words* (Garden City, NY: Doubleday, Page & Co., 1926), p. 10; Charles Dawes, *Notes as Vice President, 1928–1929* (Boston: Little, Brown, 1935), p. 30.

14. Coolidge quoted in Donald McCoy, *Calvin Coolidge: The Quiet President* (Newtown, CT: American Political Biography Press, 1998 [1967]), p. 55; McAdoo quoted in John Dean, *Warren G. Harding* (New York: Times Books, 2004), p. 73; figure of 520 in Elmer Corn-

well, "Coolidge and Presidential Leadership," *Public Opinion Quarterly* 21, no. 2 (Summer 1957), p. 272.

15. Arthur Fleser, *A Rhetorical Study of the Speaking of Calvin Coolidge* (Lewiston, NY: E. Mellen Press, 1990), p. 68. The Mencken quote is originally from *American Mercury*, March 3, 1929, p. 279.

16. Edward Lowry, "Calvin the Silent," *New Republic*, September 28, 1921, p. 129.

17. Starling, *Starling of the White House*, pp. 210–11; Alfred Pearce Dennis, "The Man Who Became President," in *Meet Calvin Coolidge: The Man Behind the Myth*, ed. Edward Lathem (Brattleboro, VT: Stephen Greene Press, 1960), p. 16; Douglas quoted in Miller, *New World Coming*, p. 124.

18. Paul Johnson, "Calvin Coolidge and the Last Arcadia," in *Calvin Coolidge and the Coolidge Era: Essays on the History of the 1920s*, ed. John Earl Haynes (Washington, DC: Library of Congress, 1998), p. 6; Michael Parrish, *Anxious Decades: America in Prosperity and Depression, 1920–1941* (New York: W. W. Norton, 1994), p. 49; Bruce Bliven, "The Great Coolidge Mystery," *Harper's Monthly*, December 1925, p. 50; Starling, *Starling of the White House*, p. 210.

19. Calvin Coolidge, *The Autobiography of Calvin Coolidge* (New York: Cosmopolitan Book Corporation, 1929), p. 184; Herbert Hoover, *Memoirs, 1920–1933*, vol. 2 (New York: Macmillan, 1952), p. 55; Baruch quoted in Robert Sobel, *Coolidge: An American Enigma* (Washington, DC: Regnery, 1998), p. 237.

20. Hull quoted in McCoy, *Quiet President*, p. 166; Coolidge quoted in Claude Fuess, *Calvin Coolidge: The Man from Vermont* (Boston: Little, Brown, 1940), p. 300; Will Rogers, "A Subtle Humorist," in Lathem, *Meet Calvin Coolidge*, p. 145.

21. Nicholas Murray Butler, *Across the Busy Years* (New York: Charles Scribner's Sons, 1939), p. 413; Oswald Garrison Villard, "Issues and Men," *Nation*, January 18, 1933, p. 55; Starling, *Starling of the White House*, p. 208.

22. Starling, *Starling of the White House*, p. 212.

23. Irwin Hoover, *Forty-two Years in the White House* (Boston: Houghton Mifflin, 1934), p. 25; Coolidge, *Autobiography*, pp. 196–97.

24. Thomas Silver, "Coolidge and the Historians," *American Scholar* 50, no. 4 (Autumn 1981), p. 514.

25. Coolidge, "Our Heritage from Hamilton," in *Price of Freedom*, pp. 109, 111; Richard Fenno, "Coolidge: Representative of the People," *Current*

History 39, no. 230 (October 1960), p. 210; William Leuchtenburg, *The Perils of Prosperity, 1914–1932* (Chicago: University of Chicago Press, 1958), p. 103.

26. *New York Times*, August 7, 1927, p. E11; *New York Times*, August 10, 1927, p. 2.

1: OUT OF PLYMOUTH NOTCH

1. Fuess, *Man from Vermont*, p. 11.
2. Coolidge, *Autobiography*, pp. 45, 29.
3. Fuess, *Man from Vermont*, p. 15.
4. Ibid., p. 23; Coolidge, *Autobiography*, p. 25.
5. Coolidge, *Autobiography*, p. 13; Starling, *Starling of the White House*, p. 212.
6. Fuess, *Man from Vermont*, p. 24.
7. Coolidge, *Autobiography*, pp. 42–43.
8. Ibid., p. 48; Fleser, *Rhetorical Study*, p. 24.
9. Coolidge, *Autobiography*, pp. 48–49.
10. Fleser, *Rhetorical Study*, p. 9; Frederick Lewis Allen, *Only Yesterday: An Informal History of the 1920s* (New York: Harper Brothers, 1931), p. 157; Coolidge, *Autobiography*, p. 66.
11. Fuess, *Man from Vermont*, p. 71.
12. Ibid., p. 73.
13. Coolidge, *Autobiography*, p. 99.
14. Starling, *Starling of the White House*, p. 219.
15. Robert Gilbert, *The Tormented President: Calvin Coolidge, Death and Clinical Depression* (Westport, CT: Praeger, 2003), p. 52; Grace Coolidge, "The Real Calvin Coolidge," *Good Housekeeping*, March 1935, p. 23.
16. Fuess, *Man from Vermont*, p. 351n.; Gilbert, *Tormented President*, pp. 48–55.
17. Coolidge, *Autobiography*, p. 94.
18. Sobel, *American Enigma*, p. 112.
19. Coolidge, *Autobiography*, p. 106.

2: ON THE BRINK

1. Bliven, "Great Coolidge Mystery," p. 49.
2. Fuess, *Man from Vermont*, p. 185.

3. The federal Volstead Act of 1920 provided for the enforcement of Prohibition but even before its passage Coolidge considered the Eighteenth Amendment to be in effect.

4. Gilbert, *Tormented President*, p. 49.

5. Fuess, *Man from Vermont*, p. 216.

6. Ibid., p. 223.

7. Calvin Coolidge, "A Telegram," September 14, 1919, in *Have Faith in Massachusetts* (Boston: Houghton Mifflin, 1919), p. 223; "Calvin Coolidge as Governor of Massachusetts" (film), FAB 888, Theodore Roosevelt Association Collection, MBRS Div., LoC; "The Policeman and Police Power," *New Republic*, October 1, 1919, p. 247.

8. Calvin Coolidge, "A Proclamation," September 24, 1919, in *Have Faith in Massachusetts*, p. 226.

9. Francis Russell, *City in Terror: Calvin Coolidge and the 1919 Boston Police Strike* (Boston: Beacon Press, 1975), p. 212.

10. Calvin Coolidge, "Plymouth, Labor Day," address delivered September 1, 1919, in *Have Faith in Massachusetts*, pp. 200–201. On examples of the progressive use of the "general interest" and similar concepts, see LeRoy Ashby, *Spearless Leader: Senator Borah and the Progressive Movement in the 1920s* (Urbana: University of Illinois Press, 1972), p. 13; Alan Dawley, *Changing the World* (Princeton, NJ: Princeton University Press, 2003), p. 68.

11. McCoy, *Quiet President*, p. 102.

12. Richard Fried, *The Man Everybody Knew: Bruce Barton and the Making of Modern America* (Chicago: Ivan R. Dee, 2005), p. 117; Bruce Barton, "Concerning Calvin Coolidge," *Collier's*, November 22, 1919, pp. 8ff.; Kerry W. Buckley, "A President for the Great Silent Majority: Bruce Barton's Construction of Calvin Coolidge," *New England Quarterly* 74, no. 4 (December 2003), p. 600.

13. McCoy, *Quiet President*, p. 99; William Allen White, *A Puritan in Babylon: The Story of Calvin Coolidge* (Norwalk, CT: The Easton Press, 1986 [1938]), p. 238; Fried, *The Man Everybody Knew*, p. 117; Barton, "Concerning Calvin Coolidge," pp. 8ff.; Bruce Barton, "Calvin Coolidge as Seen Through the Eyes of His Friends," *American Review of Reviews*, September 1923, pp. 273–78; Bruce Barton, "The Silent Man on Beacon Hill," *Woman's Home Companion*, March 1920, pp. 15ff.

14. Fuess, *Man from Vermont*, p. 197.

15. "President Harding and Calvin Coolidge," FAB 0716, Theodore Roosevelt Association Collection, MBRS Div., LoC.

16. Coolidge, *Autobiography*, p. 158; Leuchtenburg, *Perils of Prosperity*, p. 89.
17. Coolidge, *Autobiography*, p. 147.
18. Ibid., pp. 164–65.
19. Fuess, *Man from Vermont*, p. 300; Longworth, *Crowded Hours*, p. 326.
20. Fleser, *Rhetorical Study*, p. 27.
21. McCoy, *Quiet President*, p. 146.

3: THE NEW PRESIDENT

1. Allegations that Florence Harding poisoned her husband and other conspiracy theories, which have been around since the publication in 1930 of *The Strange Death of President Harding*, are baseless. See Dean, *Warren G. Harding*, pp. 164–66.
2. Coolidge, *Autobiography*, p. 180.
3. Ibid., pp. 174–75; *New York Times*, August 3, 1923, p. 1.
4. Coolidge, *Autobiography*, p. 174; White, *Puritan in Babylon*, p. 241.
5. Coolidge's sons weren't present. John was at civilian military training at Fort Devens, Massachusetts, and Calvin Jr. was working on a tobacco farm in Hatfield, near Northampton. Carrie Brown, Coolidge's stepmother, had passed away in 1920.
6. Fuess, *The Man from Vermont*, p. 314; Everett Alldredge, "Centennial History of First Congregational Church 1865–1965," available at http://www.fccuccdc.org/history.htm, accessed on May 25, 2006.
7. *New York Times*, August 15, 1923, p. 15; Coolidge, *Autobiography*, p. 183; Fuess, *Man from Vermont*, p. 320.
8. Lodge quoted in McCoy, *Quiet President*, p. 147; Norbeck quoted in Robert Ferrell, "Calvin Coolidge: The Man, the President," in Haynes, *Calvin Coolidge and the Coolidge Era*, p. 140; Harold Ickes to Henry Allen, November 24, 1923, Papers of Harold Ickes, box 29, MS Div., LoC.
9. Sobel, *American Enigma*, p. 236.
10. White, *Puritan in Babylon*, pp. 251–52.
11. Slemp, *Mind of the President*, p. 14; Longworth, *Crowded Hours*, p. 325.
12. Stephen Ponder, *Managing the Press: Origins of the Media Presidency, 1897–1933* (New York: St. Martin's Press, 1999), p. 119; Mencken, *On Politics*, pp. 132–33; John Blair, "Coolidge the Image-Maker: The President and the Press, 1923–1929," *New England Quarterly* 46, no. 4 (December 1973), p. 500.

13. Arthur Schlesinger Jr., *The Crisis of the Old Order, 1919–1933* (Boston: Houghton Mifflin, 1956), p. 51.

14. Allen, *Only Yesterday*, p. 134.

15. McCoy, *Quiet President*, p. 208.

16. Ibid., p. 212.

17. White, *Puritan in Babylon*, pp. 268–69.

18. Ibid., p. 276.

19. Lippmann, *Men of Destiny*, p. 16.

4: HITTING HIS STRIDE

1. Calvin Coolidge, "Religion and the Republic," speech delivered at the unveiling of the Equestrian Statue of Bishop Francis Asbury, Washington, DC, October 15, 1924, in *Foundations of the Republic*, p. 149; Coolidge, *Autobiography*, pp. 234–35.

2. Calvin Coolidge, "The Spiritual Unification of America," speech at the laying of the cornerstone of the Jewish Community Center, Washington, DC, May 3, 1925, in *Foundations of the Republic*, pp. 209–18.

3. Grace Coolidge, "A Wife Remembers," in Lathem, *Meet Calvin Coolidge*, pp. 65–66; Jules Abels, *In the Time of Silent Cal* (New York: G. P. Putnam's Sons, 1969), p. 39; Gamaliel Bradford, *The Quick and the Dead* (Boston: Houghton Mifflin, 1931), p. 227.

4. Starling, *Starling of the White House*, p. 80; *New York Times*, March 1, 1925, p. XX1; Hoover, *Forty-two Years in the White House*, pp. 262, 268, 323; Appointment books, Calvin Coolidge Papers, boxes 289–92, MS Div., LoC.

5. Coolidge, *Autobiography*, pp. 201–2; Starling, *Starling of the White House*, p. 209; McCoy, *The Quiet President*, p. 159.

6. Hoover, *Forty-two Years in the White House*, pp. 132, 238; Coolidge, *Autobiography*, p. 200; Starling, *Starling of the White House*, p. 207; Fuess, *Man from Vermont*, p. 5; McCoy, *Quiet President*, p. 177; Stephen Schuker, "American Foreign Policy: The European Dimension," in Haynes, *Calvin Coolidge and the Coolidge Era*, p. 291.

7. Abels, *Silent Cal*, p. 182; Daniel Leab, "Coolidge, Hays, and 1920 Movies: Some Aspects of Image and Reality," in Haynes, *Calvin Coolidge and the Coolidge Era*, p. 103.

8. Hoover, *Forty-two Years in the White House*, p. 13; James Coupal, "Football 'Medicine,'" *Good Housekeeping*, March 1935, p. 219; Fuess, *Man from Vermont*, p. 23.

9. Hoover, *Forty-two Years in the White House*, p. 290; Fuess, *Man from Vermont*, p. 490; Starling, *Starling of the White House*, p. 79; Gilbert, *Tormented President*, pp. 46–47, 217.

10. Hoover, *Forty-two Years in the White House*, pp. 132, 233; Starling, *Starling of the White House*, p. 255.

11. "People," *Time*, May 16, 1955.

12. Quoted in White, *Puritan in Babylon*, p. 257.

13. Slemp, *The Mind of the President*, pp. 12–13; Herbert Hoover, *Memoirs*, pp. 55–56.

14. "The Danger of Too Much Coolidge," *New Republic*, December 26, 1923, p. 109.

15. White, *Puritan in Babylon*, p. 261; Coolidge, *Autobiography*, p. 229.

16. Fleser, *A Rhetorical Study*, p. 28; Coolidge, *Autobiography*, pp. 219–20.

17. Blair, "Coolidge the Image-Maker," p. 502; Ponder, *Managing the Press*, p. 109.

18. Cornwell, "Coolidge and Presidential Leadership," p. 272; *New York Times*, August 7, 1927, p. XX11.

19. Lindsay Rogers, "The White House 'Spokesman,'" *Virginia Quarterly Review* (July 1926), p. 366; Coolidge, *Autobiography*, p. 184; Cornwell, "Coolidge and Presidential Leadership," p. 274. For samples of the questions themselves, see Calvin Coolidge Papers, reel 39, case 36, MS Div., LoC.

20. Sobel, *American Enigma*, p. 240; Starling, *Starling of the White House*, p. 234.

21. Blair, "Coolidge the Image-Maker," p. 504; Calvin Coolidge Papers, reel 54, case 72, MS Div., LoC.

22. "President Coolidge: Taken on the White House Grounds," FEC 4575, AFI/Maurice Zouary Collection, MBRS Div., LoC ; *New York Times*, April 22, 1925, p. 8; "Visitin' 'Round at Coolidge Corners" [Patheb4 News], FEB 8580, AFI/Harold Casselton/Ted Larson Collection, MBRS Div., LoC; Abels, *Silent Cal*, pp. 191–92. On the De Forest exchange, see Calvin Coolidge Papers, reel 54, case 72, MS Div., LoC.

23. Blair, "Coolidge the Image-Maker," p. 521; Clark quoted in Gil Troy, *See How They Ran: The Changing Role of the Presidential Candidate*, 2d ed., rev. (Cambridge, MA: Harvard University Press, 1996 [1991]), p. 149; Leab, "Coolidge, Hays, and 1920s Movies," p. 102.

24. Rogers quoted in Ponder, *Managing the Press*, p. 123; Denny quoted in John Tebbel and Sarah Miles Watts, *The Press and the Presidency:*

From George Washington to Ronald Reagan (New York: Oxford University Press, 1985), p. 406.

25. Blair, "Coolidge the Image-Maker," pp. 500–501.

5: THE COOLIDGE PROSPERITY

1. George Soule, *Prosperity Decade: From War to Depression, 1917–1929* (White Plains, NY: M. E. Sharpe, 1975 [1947]), pp. 3, 132. Soule notes that some of the burden was shifted to local governments, which in the 1920s cumulatively ran deficits that offset the new federal surplus.

2. Ann Douglas, *Terrible Honesty: Mongrel Manhattan in the 1920s* (New York: Farrar, Straus and Giroux, 1995), p. 434.

3. Bryan quoted in Raymond Vickers, *Panic in Paradise: Florida's Banking Crash of 1926* (Tuscaloosa: University of Alabama Press, 1994), p. 19; Allen, *Only Yesterday*, p. 138.

4. Slemp, *The Mind of the President*, p. 11.

5. Andrew Mellon, *Taxation: The People's Business* (New York: Macmillan, 1924).

6. *New York Times*, February 13, 1924, p. 1. Historian David Shreve has found that the term "trickle down" came into use in 1932 as a criticism liberals used against the newly created Reconstruction Finance Corporation and, retroactively, Mellon's economics. Shreve also notes that William Jennings Bryan used a variant of the concept in his 1896 speech at the Democratic National Convention: "There are those who believe that, if you will only legislate to make the well-to-do prosperous, their prosperity will leak through on those below. The Democratic idea, however, has been that if you legislate to make the masses prosperous, their prosperity will find its way up through every class which rests upon them."

7. Sidney Ratner, *Taxation and Democracy in America* (New York: John Wiley, 1967 [1942]), pp. 406–12, 417. The major boon to corporations was the 1921 elimination of the World War I–era excess profits tax, a type of burden imposed on companies in war or emergencies.

8. *New York Times*, December 7, 1927, p. 24. One critic of Mellon's, Huey Long of Louisiana, would give vent to this outrage in a 1932 Senate speech. "Mr. Mellon," Long declared, "points out that this is a grave condition; that the law has been miraculously at fault in failing to collect an income tax against a larger percentage of the people. . . .

It is the infernal fact that 98 percent of the people of the United States have nothing, rather than it being the fault of the fact that only 2 percent of them pay any income tax." Henry Christian, ed., *Kingfish to America: Share Our Wealth: Selected Senatorial Papers of Huey P. Long* (New York: Schocken Books, 1985), pp. 13–14.

9. Silas Bent, *Strange Bedfellows: A Review of Politics, Personalities, and the Press* (New York: Horace Liveright, 1928), pp. xii–xiii; Bruce Barton, *The Man Nobody Knows: A Discovery of Jesus* (Indianapolis: Bobbs-Merrill, 1925); Mencken quoted in Parrish, *Anxious Decades*, p. 29.

10. Humphrey quoted in Schlesinger, *Crisis of the Old Order*, p. 65.

11. Kriste Lindenmeyer, *A Right to Childhood: The U.S. Children's Bureau and Child Welfare, 1912–46* (Urbana: University of Illinois Press, 1997), p. 100; Lela Costin, *Two Sisters for Social Justice: A Biography of Grace and Edith Abbott* (Urbana: University of Illinois Press, 1983), p. 147.

12. *New York Times*, November 24, 1923, p. 12; Harold Ickes to Henry Allen, November 24, 1923, Papers of Harold Ickes, box 29, MS Div., LoC.

13. *New York Times*, December 7, 1923, p. 3; Jeffrey Tulis, *The Rhetorical Presidency* (Princeton, NJ: Princeton University Press, 1987), p. 118.

14. Fuess, *Man from Vermont*, p. 334.

15. S. K. Ratcliffe, "President Coolidge's Triumph," *Contemporary Review* (July 1924), p. 705; Hoover, *Forty-two Years in the White House*, pp. 127–28.

16. McCoy, *Quiet President*, p. 202; *New York Times*, March 8, 1924, p. 1; *New York Times*, February 15, 1924, p. 1.

17. *New York Times*, May 4, 1924, p. 1; *New York Times*, May 16, 1924, p. 1; *New York Times*, May 20, 1924, p. 1.

18. *New York Times*, January 5, 1924, p. 1; *New York Times*, March 28, 1924, p. 19.

19. *New York Times*, June 6, 1924, p. 1. The top surtaxes affected those earning at least $500,000 ($5.9 million in 2006 dollars) and the threshold for having to pay surtaxes was raised to $10,000 ($118,000 in 2006 dollars).

6: CONTROVERSIES

1. The term "political fundamentalism" comes from Leuchtenburg, *The Perils of Prosperity*, pp. 204–24.

2. Marvin Olasky and John Perry, *Monkey Business: The True Story of the Scopes Trial* (Nashville: Broadmant Holmar, 2005), p. 16.

3. Calvin Coolidge, "Toleration and Liberalism," address before the American Legion Convention at Omaha, Nebraska, October 6, 1925, in *Foundations of the Republic*, p. 298; Calvin Coolidge, "Whose Country Is This?" *Good Housekeeping*, February 1935, p. 14, cited in John Higham, *Strangers in the Land: Patterns of American Nativism, 1865–1920* (New Brunswick, NJ: Rutgers University Press, 1955), p. 318.

4. McCoy, *Quiet President*, p. 230.

5. *New York Times*, August 17, 1923, p. 2; *New York Times*, October 12, 1924, p. 2; Dawes, *Notes as Vice President*, pp. 22–25; Ratcliffe, "President Coolidge's Triumph," p. 710; Coolidge, "Toleration and Liberalism, pp. 287–301. Vice-presidential nominee Charles Dawes also criticized the Klan and claimed that Coolidge commended him for his remarks afterward.

6. *New York Times*, December 7, 1923, p. 4.

7. Barton, "Calvin Coolidge as Seen Through the Eyes of His Friends," p. 277; Kenneth O'Reilly, *Nixon's Piano: Presidents and Racial Politics from Washington to Clinton* (New York: Free Press, 1995), pp. 98–99; Matthew Rees, *From the Deck to the Sea: Blacks and the Republican Party* (Wakefield, NH: Longwood Academic, 1991), p. 125.

8. Howard Quint and Robert Ferrell, eds., *The Talkative President: The Off-the-Record Press Conferences of Calvin Coolidge* (Amherst: University of Massachusetts Press, 1964), p. 176.

9. *New York Times*, October 17, 1925, p. 1.

10. Frank Kent, "Mr. Coolidge," *American Mercury*, August 1924, p. 389, reprinted as "The Press and Mr. Coolidge," in *New Republic*, June 13, 1960, p. 14; Dawes quoted in Fleser, *Rhetorical Study*, p. 51.

7: GETTING ELECTED

1. *New York Times*, August 4, 1923, p. 1.

2. Fuess, *Man from Vermont*, p. 335.

3. *New York Times*, December 20, 1923, pp. 1, 16.

4. Gilbert, *Tormented President*, pp. 151–52.

5. Ibid, p. 153; Dawes quoted in Sobel, *American Enigma*, p. 295.

6. White, *Puritan in Babylon*, p. 308.

7. Starling, *Starling of the White House*, p. 221.

8. Coolidge, *Autobiography*, p. 190.

9. *New York Times*, July 9, 1924, p. 19.

10. Gilbert, *Tormented President*, pp. 160, 163. Gilbert, from whose monograph *The Tormented President* (2003) this account draws,

broke ground in reconstructing the events surrounding Calvin Jr.'s death by examining the papers of Joel Boone, the White House physician. Gilbert concluded that Coolidge became clinically depressed after his son's death and that the president's governance changed starkly after the boy's death. Valuable as Gilbert's book is, his diagnosis of clinical depression is speculative. As Gilbert acknowledges, Coolidge's shyness and laconic style were lifelong traits—making the continuities in his character before and after the boy's passing seem more salient than any changes.

11. John Lambert, "When the President Wept," *Good Housekeeping*, March 1935, pp. 225–26; Fuess, *Man from Vermont*, p. 351; Starling, *Starling of the White House*, p. 224.

12. Coolidge, *Autobiography*, pp. 190–91.

13. Bruce Barton to Edward T. Clark, December 12, 1923, Clark Papers, box 1, folder 8, MS Div., LoC; Barton to Frank W. Stearns, December 31, 1923, Clark Papers, box 1, folder 8, MS Div., LoC; Barton, "Calvin Coolidge as Seen Through the Eyes of His Friends," pp. 273–78; *New York Times*, October 20, 1962, pp. 1, 15; Terry Hynes, "Media Manipulation and Political Campaigns: Bruce Barton and the Presidential Elections of the Jazz Age," *Journalism History* 4, no. 3 (Autumn 1977), p. 94; Fried, *Man Everybody Knew*, pp. 90, 123.

14. Quint and Ferrell, *Talkative President*, p. 47; Douglas Craig, *Fireside Politics: Radio and Political Culture in the United States, 1920–1940* (Baltimore: Johns Hopkins University Press, 2000), p. 142.

15. Clark quoted in Troy, *See How They Ran*, p. 148; McCoy, *Quiet President*, pp. 254–55.

16. *New York Times*, September 2, 1927, p. XX11; Cornwell, "Coolidge and Presidential Leadership," p. 267; on phonograph records see Calvin Coolidge Papers, reel 90, case 177, MS Div., LoC.

17. Craig, *Fireside Politics*, p. 142; Slemp, *The Mind of the President*, p. 10; Cornwell, "Coolidge and Presidential Leadership," pp. 268–70.

18. Craig, *Fireside Politics*, p. 145; *New York Times*, July 18, 1924, p. 3.

19. *New York Times*, August 15, 1924, p. 2.

20. Buckley, "A President for the 'Great Silent Majority,'" p. 616.

21. *New York Times*, August 20, 1924, p. 3; McCoy, *Quiet President*, pp. 255–56.

22. *New York Times*, October 18, 1924, p. 1; Edward Bernays, "Manipulating Public Opinion: The Why and the How," *American Journal of Sociology* 33, no. 6 (May 1928), p. 967; Larry Tye, *The Father of Spin:*

Edward L. Bernays and the Birth of Public Relations (New York: Henry Holt, 1998), pp. 78–79.

23. Tye, *Father of Spin*, pp. 77–78; Buckley, "A President for the 'Great Silent Majority,'" p. 617.

24. Craig, *Fireside Politics*, pp. 144–45; Leab, "Coolidge, Hays, and 1920s Movies," p. 102; McCoy, *Quiet President*, p. 262; Bliven, "Great Coolidge Mystery," p. 50.

25. Troy, *See How They Ran*, pp. 147–48; Bliven, "Great Coolidge Mystery," p. 50.

26. David Burner, "Election of 1924," in *History of American Presidential Elections, 1789–1968*, vol. 6, ed. Arthur Schlesinger Jr. and Fred Israel (New York: Chelsea House, 1985) p. 2485; McCoy, *Quiet President*, p. 260.

27. Oswald Garrison Villard, *Fighting Years: Memoirs of a Liberal Editor* (New York: Harcourt, Brace, 1939), pp. 497–98; Chester Rowell, "Why I Shall Vote for Coolidge," *New Republic*, October 29, 1924, pp. 219–21.

28. Kenneth Roberts, "Calvin Coolidge, Politician," in Lathem, *Meet Calvin Coolidge*, p. 31.

29. Bliven, "Great Coolidge Mystery," p. 45.

8: BEYOND AMERICA'S SHORES

1. McCoy, *Quiet President*, p. 264; Hoover, *Forty-two Years in the White House*, p. 141. The State, War, and Navy Building was later renamed the Old Executive Office Building.

2. Butler, *Across the Busy Years*, p. 358.

3. McCoy, *Quiet President*, p. 279; Starling, *Starling of the White House*, p. 228. The rejected nominee was Andrew Johnson's choice for attorney general, Henry Stanbery.

4. Quint and Ferrell, *Talkative President*, p. 96.

5. George Nash, "The 'Great Enigma' and the 'Great Engineer,'" in Haynes, *Calvin Coolidge and the Coolidge Era*, pp. 149–90; T.R.B., "Washington Notes," *New Republic*, September 2, 1925, p. 43.

6. Fuess, *Man from Vermont*, p. 406; Schuker, "American Foreign Policy," p. 292.

7. Fuess, *Man from Vermont*, p. 405; *New York Times*, December 7, 1923, p. 4.

8. *New York Times*, December 7, 1923, p. 4.

9. Quint and Ferrell, *Talkative President*, p. 157.

10. *New York Times*, December 4, 1924, p. 8; Michael Dunne, *The United States and the World Court, 1920–1935* (New York: St. Martin's Press, 1988), pp. 99–101.

11. *New York Times*, April 26, 1925, p. 1; L. Ethan Ellis, *Frank B. Kellogg and American Foreign Relations* (New Brunswick, NJ: Rutgers University Press, 1961), p. 226.

12. McCoy, *Quiet President*, p. 362; Quint and Ferrell, *Talkative President*, p. 208; *New York Times*, January 28, 1926, p. 1.

13. Quint and Ferrell, *Talkative President*, p. 209.

14. Dunne, *United States and World Court*, p. 169.

15. Ibid., p. 69.

16. *New York Times*, September 1, 1923, p. 1; McCoy, *Quiet President*, pp. 178–79.

17. Ellis, *Frank B. Kellogg*, pp. 59–60.

18. Quint and Ferrell, *Talkative President*, pp. 239–40.

19. Bliven, "Great Coolidge Mystery," p. 49; McCoy, *Quiet President*, pp. 355–56.

20. Calvin Coolidge, "Message on Nicaragua," in *Calvin Coolidge, 1872–1933: Chronology—Documents—Bibliographical Aids*, ed. Philip Moran (Dobbs Ferry, NY: Oceana Publications, 1970), p. 86.

21. Ellis, *Frank B. Kellogg*, p. 73.

22. Ibid., p. 99.

23. Like many policies of the era, the treaties would later draw fire. By committing the United States to limit the defenses of its Pacific Island holdings, and by surrendering American supremacy, they arguably encouraged Japanese aggression in Asia in the 1930s. At the time, however, the pacts were praised for embodying precisely the kind of bold strides toward peace that Wilson had failed to attain.

24. Quint and Ferrell, *Talkative President*, p. 215.

25. McCoy, *Quiet President*, p. 375.

26. *New York Times*, December 5, 1928, p. 26.

27. Parrish, *Anxious Decades*, p. 60.

9: HIGH TIDE OF REPUBLICANISM

1. *New York Times*, June 7, 1927, p. 8.; *New York Times*, June 11, 1927, p. 3.

2. Merz quoted in Allen, *Only Yesterday*, p. 189; *New York Times*, June 12,

1927, p. 2; *New York Times,* June 3, 1927, p. 1; *New York Times,* June 13, 1927, p. 8; *New York Times,* June 19, 1927, p. X3.

3. *New York Times,* June 12, 1927, p. 8; *New York Times,* June 13, 1927, p. 2.

4. John Ward, "The Meaning of Lindbergh's Flight," *American Quarterly* 10, no.1 (Spring 1958), p. 7; Mullet quoted in Parrish, *Anxious Decades,* p. 179; *New Republic* quoted in Ward, p. 6. Contrary to lore, Lindbergh was not the first man to traverse the Atlantic. A handful of others had done so—traveling from Newfoundland, Canada, to Ireland, or along other routes—though none had gone the full distance of New York to Paris.

5. Ratner, *Taxation and Democracy,* p. 424; David Burner, *The Politics of Provincialism: The Democratic Party in Transition* (Cambridge, MA: Harvard University Press, 1986 [1967]), p. 165; *New York Times,* March 7, 1926, p. 14.

6. Quint and Ferrell, *Talkative President,* p. 98.

7. William MacDonald, " 'Coolidge Prosperity' a Campaign Issue," *Current History* (November 1926), pp. 248–50; *New York Times,* October 29, 1926, pp. 1, 20.

8. Bruce Barton to Calvin Coolidge, undated, Edward T. Clark Papers, box 1, folder 8, MS Div., LoC; Edward T. Clark to Bruce Barton, October 2, 1926, Edward T. Clark Papers, box 1, folder 8, MS Div., LoC.

9. Calvin Coolidge to Edward T. Clark, October 28, 1932, Clark Papers, box 2, folder "Calvin Coolidge #3," MS Div., LoC; *New York Times,* September 23, 1926, p. 4.

10. *New York Times,* September 28, 1926, p. 27; Fried, *The Man Everybody Knew,* p. 126; Frank W. Stearns to Edward T. Clark, September 30, 1926, Clark Papers, box 17, folder "Stearns," MS Div., LoC.

11. McCoy, *Quiet President,* p. 313.

12. *New York Times,* December 8, 1926, p 14.

13. Ibid.

14. Craig, *Fireside Politics,* pp. 66–68.

15. Ibid., p. 57.

16. John Barry, *Rising Tide: The Great Mississippi Flood of 1927* (New York: Simon & Schuster, 1997), pp. 286–87; Matthew Pearcy, "After the Flood: A History of the 1928 Flood Control Act," *Journal of the Illinois State Historical Society* (Summer 2002). Online at http://www.findarticles.com/p/articles/mi_qa3945/is_200207/ai_n9105154/, viewed on June 4, 2006.

17. Barry, *Rising Tide*, p. 369.
18. Ibid., pp. 372–73.
19. Pearcy, "After the Flood"; Barry, *Rising Tide*, pp. 405–6.
20. Quint and Ferrell, *Talkative President*, pp. 81–82; Pearcy, "After the Flood."
21. Pearcy, "After the Flood"; Barry, *Rising Tide*, p. 406.
22. Blair, "Coolidge the Image-Maker," p. 522; White, *Puritan in Babylon*, p. 352.
23. *New York Times*, July 5, 1927, pp. 1, 3; Fuess, *Man from Vermont*, p. 391; *New York Times*, June 19, 1927, p. 16; Hoover, *Forty-two Years in the White House*, p. 168.
24. Fuess, *Man from Vermont*, pp. 392–93.
25. Ibid., pp. 393–94.
26. Ibid., p. 394.
27. White, *Puritan in Babylon*, p. 360.
28. Ibid., p. 361.
29. Ibid., p. 360.
30. Coolidge, *Autobiography*, pp. 242, 244; White, *Puritan in Babylon*, p. 366n; Starling, *Starling of the White House*, p. 249. One oft-repeated secondhand account has Grace Coolidge stating, "Poppa says a depression is coming," but the first lady denied ever making the comment.
31. Coolidge, *Autobiography*, p. 241; Starling, *Starling of the White House*, p. 249.
32. Starling, *Starling of the White House*, p. 263.

10: A CONTESTED LEGACY

1. Hoover, *Forty-two Years in the White House*, p. 180.
2. *New York Times*, December 5, 1928, p. 26; Herbert Hoover, *Memoirs*, vol. 3, p. 16.
3. Bliven, "Great Coolidge Mystery," p. 51; Al Smith, "A Shining Example," in Lathem, *Meet Calvin Coolidge*, p. 220; Holmes quoted in McCoy, *Quiet President*, pp. 262–63.
4. Allen, *Only Yesterday*, p. 252; Michael Bernstein, "The Great Depression as a Historical Problem," in *The Economics of the Great Depression*, ed. Mark Wheeler (Kalamazoo, MI: W. E. Upjohn Institute for Employment Research, 1998), p. 66.
5. Soule, *Prosperity Decade*, pp. 317, 326, 328; John Kenneth Galbraith, *The Great Crash, 1929* (New York: Mariner Books, 1997 [1954]), pp. 173–74.

6. John Maynard Keynes, *The General Theory of Employment, Interest, and Money* (London: Macmillan, 1936), p. 151.
7. Schlesinger, *Crisis of the Old Order,* pp. 134–36; Alan Brinkley, *The End of Reform* (New York: Alfred A. Knopf, 1995), pp. 74–77.
8. Hoover quoted in Allen, *Only Yesterday,* p. 263; Mellon quoted in Galbraith, *Great Crash,* p. 15; Frank Kent, "The Democrats Stand by Mellon," *Nation,* March 17, 1926, pp. 281–82; Leuchtenburg, *Perils of Prosperity,* p. 242.
9. Leuchtenburg, *Perils of Prosperity,* p. 243; Allen, *Only Yesterday,* pp. 268–73.
10. Leuchtenburg, *Perils of Prosperity,* p. 246.
11. Galbraith, *Great Crash,* p. 1.
12. Parrish, *Anxious Decades,* p. 230.
13. Galbraith, *Great Crash,* p. 21; *New York Times,* January 7, 1928, p. 2; *New York Times,* January 8, 1928, p. 43.
14. Galbraith, *Great Crash,* p. 34. If the Fed failed to stop the reckless investing early on, it waited until too late to rein it in. In August 1929, after Coolidge left office, the Fed voted to raise interest rates again, to 6 percent. The move contracted the money supply just when the economy was entering recession. The deflationary effects kicked in after the crash, precisely when a more stimulative policy was needed.
15. White, *Puritan in Babylon,* p. 422; Fuess, *Man from Vermont,* p. 456; Calvin Coolidge to Edward T. Clark, March 26, 1932, Clark Papers, box 2, folder "Calvin Coolidge #3," MS Div., LoC.
16. Fuess, *Man from Vermont,* p. 455; White, *Puritan in Babylon,* p. 415; McCoy, *Quiet President,* pp. 394, 398.
17. *New York Times,* November 10, 1929, p. BR9.
18. Grace Coolidge to Edward T. Clark, March 16, 1935, Clark Papers, LoC MS Division, box 2, folder "Calvin Coolidge #5," MS Div., LoC.
19. Edward T. Clark to Bruce Barton, January 26, 1933, Clark Papers, box 1, folder 8, MS Div., LoC.
20. White, *Puritan in Babylon,* p. 427.
21. Matthew Josephson, "The 'New Era': Its Rise and Fall," *New Republic,* November 4, 1931, p. 315; Mencken, *On Politics,* p. 140.
22. Starling, *Starling of the White House,* p. 302; Clark to Barton, January 26, 1933 Clark Papers, MS Div., LoC.
23. Henry Stoddard, "I No Longer Fit In," in Lathem, *Meet Calvin Coolidge,* p. 214.
24. *New York Times,* May 20, 1928, p. 74.

25. Slemp, *The Mind of the President*, p. 11; Fenno, "Coolidge Representative," p. 208; Fuess, *Man from Vermont*, p. 334.
26. Cather quoted in Lynn Dumenil, *The Modern Temper: American Culture and Society in the 1920s* (New York: Hill & Wang, 1995), p. 3.
27. Mencken, *On Politics*, p. 140.

Milestones

1872	Born July 4, Plymouth Notch, Vermont
1885	Victoria Moor Coolidge, mother, dies at age thirty-nine
1890	Abigail Coolidge, sister, dies at age fourteen
	Graduates from Black River Academy, Ludlow, Vermont
1895	Graduates from Amherst College
1897	Admitted to the bar in Massachusetts
1905	Marries Grace Goodhue, Burlington, Vermont
1906	Son John Coolidge is born
1908	Son Calvin Coolidge Jr. is born
1909	Elected mayor of Northampton, Massachusetts
1915	Elected lieutenant governor of Massachusetts
1918	Elected governor of Massachusetts
1919	Elevated to national prominence during Boston police strike
1920	Elected vice president of the United States, running with Warren G. Harding
1923	Becomes president on August 2 upon Harding's death
	Delivers State of the Union address to Congress
1924	Appoints prosecutors to investigate Harding scandals
	Signs first Coolidge-Mellon tax bill
	Signs Johnson-Reed Immigration Act
	Approves Dawes Plan
	Veterans' bonus passes over Coolidge's veto
	Calvin Jr., son, dies at age sixteen of bacterial infection acquired after playing tennis on White House lawn
	Elected president with 54 percent of the popular vote

1925   First president to appear in talking film
         Appoints Harlan Fiske Stone to Supreme Court
1926   Senate approves World Court membership, with reservations
         Signs second Coolidge-Mellon tax bill
         John Coolidge, father, dies at age eighty
         Democratic gains in off-year elections
1927   Mississippi River flood
         Signs Radio Act
         Vetoes McNary-Haugen bill for first time
         Awards Charles Lindbergh Distinguished Flying Cross
         Fails at naval disarmament conference in Geneva
         Announces plans to retire from presidency after his term is up
         Stock market speculation heats up
1928   Address to Pan-American Conference, Havana
         Signs third Coolidge-Mellon tax bill, flood-control bill
         Vetoes McNary-Haugen bill for second time
         Kellogg-Briand Pact
         Herbert Hoover elected president
1929   Retires to Northampton
         Publishes *Autobiography of Calvin Coolidge*
         Stock market crash
1930   Begins writing syndicated newspaper column
1932   Franklin D. Roosevelt elected president
1933   Dies January 5, Northampton, Massachusetts, age sixty

Bibliography

MANUSCRIPT COLLECTIONS

Motion Picture, Broadcasting and Recorded Sound Division, Library of Congress, Washington, DC.
Edward T. Clark Papers, Manuscript Division, Library of Congress, Washington, DC.
Calvin Coolidge Papers, Manuscript Division, Library of Congress, Washington, DC.
Harold Ickes Papers, Manuscript Division, Library of Congress, Washington, DC.

BOOKS: PRIMARY SOURCES

Butler, Nicholas Murray. *Across the Busy Years: Recollections and Reflections.* New York: Charles Scribner's Sons, 1939.
Christian, Henry, ed. *Kingfish to America: Share Our Wealth: Selected Senatorial Papers of Huey P. Long.* New York: Schocken Books, 1985.
Coolidge, Calvin. *The Autobiography of Calvin Coolidge.* New York: Cosmopolitan Book Corporation, 1929.
———. *Foundations of the Republic: Speeches and Addresses.* New York: Charles Scribner's Sons, 1926.
———. *Have Faith in Massachusetts.* Boston: Houghton Mifflin, 1919.
———. *The Price of Freedom: Speeches and Addresses.* New York: Charles Scribner's Sons, 1924.
Dawes, Charles. *Notes as Vice President.* Boston: Little, Brown, 1935.
Hoover, Herbert. *Memoirs.* 3 vols. New York: Macmillan, 1951–52.

Hoover, Irwin. *Forty-two Years in the White House.* Boston: Houghton Mifflin, 1934.

Lathem, Edward Connery, ed. *Meet Calvin Coolidge: The Man Behind the Myth.* Brattleboro, VT: Stephen Greene Press, 1960.

Longworth, Alice Roosevelt. *Crowded Hours.* New York: Charles Scribner's Sons, 1933.

Mellon, Andrew. *Taxation: The People's Business.* New York: Macmillan, 1924.

Moran, Philip, ed. *Calvin Coolidge, 1872–1933: Chronology—Documents—Bibliographical Aids.* Dobbs Ferry, NY: Oceana Publications, 1970.

Quint, Howard, and Robert Ferrell, eds. *The Talkative President: The Off-the-Record Press Conferences of Calvin Coolidge.* Amherst: University of Massachusetts Press, 1964.

Reagan, Ronald. *An American Life.* New York: Simon & Schuster, 1990.

Skinner, Kiron, Annelise Anderson, and Martin Anderson, eds. *Reagan: A Life in Letters.* New York: Free Press, 2003.

Slemp, C. Bascom. *The Mind of the President: As Revealed by Himself in His Own Words.* Garden City, NY: Doubleday, Page & Co, 1926.

Smith, Ira, with Joe Alex Morris. *Dear Mr. President: The Story of Fifty Years in the White House Mail Room.* New York: Julian Messner, 1949.

Starling, Edmund. *Starling of the White House.* New York: Simon & Schuster, 1946.

Villard, Oswald Garrison. *Fighting Years: Memoirs of a Liberal Editor.* New York: Harcourt, Brace, 1939.

BOOKS: SECONDARY SOURCES

Abels, Jules. *In the Time of Silent Cal.* New York: G. P. Putnam's Sons, 1969.

Allen, Frederick Lewis. *Only Yesterday: An Informal History of the 1920s.* New York: Harper Brothers, 1931.

Ashby, LeRoy. *Spearless Leader: Senator Borah and the Progressive Movement in the 1920s.* Urbana: University of Illinois Press, 1972.

Barry, John. *Rising Tide: The Great Mississippi Flood of 1927.* New York: Simon & Schuster, 1997.

Barnuow, Erik. *A Tower in Babel: A History of Broadcasting in the United States to 1933.* New York: Oxford University Press, 1978 [1966].

Barton, Bruce. *The Man Nobody Knows: A Discovery of Jesus.* Indianapolis: Bobbs-Merrill, 1925.

Bent, Silas. *Strange Bedfellows: A Review of Politics, Personalities, and the Press.* New York: Horace Liveright, 1928.

Bernstein, Irving. *The Lean Years: A History of the American Worker, 1920–1933.* Baltimore: Penguin Books, 1966.

Booraem, Hendrik. *The Provincial: Calvin Coolidge and His World, 1885–1895.* Lewisburg, PA: Bucknell University Press, 1994.

Bradford, Gamaliel. *The Quick and the Dead.* Boston: Houghton Mifflin, 1931.

Brinkley, Alan. *The End of Reform: New Deal Liberalism in Recession and War.* New York: Alfred A. Knopf, 1995.

Brownlee, W. Elliot. *Dynamics of Ascent: A History of the American Economy.* 2nd ed. New York: Alfred A. Knopf, 1988 [1974].

Burner, David. *The Politics of Provincialism: The Democratic Party in Transition, 1918–1932.* New York: Alfred A. Knopf, 1968.

Cannadine, David. *Mellon: An American Life.* New York: Alfred A. Knopf, 2006.

Costin, Lela. *Two Sisters for Social Justice: A Biography of Grace and Edith Abbott.* Urbana: University of Illinois Press, 1983.

Cott, Nancy. *The Grounding of Modern Feminism.* New Haven: Yale University Press, 1977.

Craig, Douglas. *Fireside Politics: Radio and Political Culture in the United States, 1920–1940.* Baltimore: Johns Hopkins University Press, 2000.

Dawley, Alan. *Changing the World: American Progressives in War and Revolution.* Princeton, NJ: Princeton University Press, 2003.

Dean, John. *Warren G. Harding.* New York: Times Books, 2004.

Douglas, Ann. *Terrible Honesty: Mongrel Manhattan in the 1920s.* New York: Farrar, Straus and Giroux, 1995.

Dumenil, Lynn. *The Modern Temper: American Culture and Society in the 1920s.* New York: Hill & Wang, 1995.

Dunne, Michael. *The United States and the World Court, 1920–1935.* New York: St. Martin's Press, 1988.

Ellis, L. Ethan. *Frank B. Kellogg and American Foreign Relations.* New Brunswick, NJ: Rutgers University Press, 1961.

Fass, Paula. *The Damned and the Beautiful: American Youth in the 1920s.* New York: Oxford University Press, 1977.

Ferrell, Robert. *The Presidency of Calvin Coolidge.* Lawrence: University Press of Kansas, 1998.

Fitzgerald, F. Scott. *The Beautiful and the Damned.* New York: Penguin Putnam, 1998.

Fleser, Arthur. *A Rhetorical Study of the Speaking of Calvin Coolidge.* Lewiston, NY: E. Mellen Press, 1990.

Fox, Richard Wightman, and Jackson Lears, eds. *The Culture of Consumption: Critical Essays in American History, 1880–1980.* New York: Pantheon Books, 1983.

Fried, Richard. *The Man Everybody Knew: Bruce Barton and the Making of Modern America.* Chicago: Ivan R. Dee, 2005.

Fuess, Claude. *Calvin Coolidge, the Man from Vermont.* Boston: Little, Brown, 1940.

Galbraith, John Kenneth. *The Great Crash, 1929.* New York: Mariner Books, 1997 [1954].

Gilbert, Robert. *The Tormented President: Calvin Coolidge, Death and Clinical Depression.* Westport, CT: Praeger, 2003.

Hawley, Ellis. *The Great War and the Search for a Modern Order: A History of the American People and Their Institutions.* New York: St. Martin's Press, 1979.

Haynes, John Earl, ed. *Calvin Coolidge and the Coolidge Era: Essays on the History of the 1920s.* Washington, DC: Library of Congress, 1998.

Higham, John. *Strangers in the Land: Patterns of American Nativism, 1865–1920.* New Brunswick, NJ: Rutgers University Press, 1955.

Hofstadter, Richard. *The Age of Reform: From Bryan to F.D.R.* New York: Vintage Books, 1955.

Kernell, Samuel. *Going Public: New Strategies of Presidential Leadership.* Washington, DC: CQ Press, 1986.

Keynes, John Maynard. *The General Theory of Employment, Interest, and Money.* London: Macmillan, 1936.

Lears, Jackson. *Fables of Abundance: A Cultural History of Advertising in America.* New York: Basic Books, 1994.

Leopold, Richard. *Elihu Root and the Conservative Tradition.* Boston: Little, Brown, 1954.

Leuchtenburg, William. *The Perils of Prosperity, 1914–1932.* Chicago: University of Chicago Press, 1958.

Lewis, Sinclair. *The Man Who Knew Coolidge.* New York: Harcourt, Brace, 1928.

Lindenmeyer, Kriste. *A Right to Childhood: The U.S. Children's Bureau and Child Welfare, 1912–46.* Urbana: University of Illinois Press, 1997.

Lippmann, Walter. *Liberty and the News.* New York: Harcourt, Brace, and Howe, 1920.

———. *Men of Destiny.* New York: Macmillan, 1927.

Lynd, Robert, and Helen Merrell Lynd. *Middletown: A Study in Modern American Culture.* New York: Harcourt, Brace & World, 1956 [1929].

Marchand, Roland. *Advertising the American Dream: Making Way for Modernity, 1920–1940.* Berkeley: University of California Press, 1985.

McCoy, Donald. *Calvin Coolidge: The Quiet President.* Newtown, CT: American Political Biography Press, 1998 [1967].

Mencken, H. L. *On Politics: A Carnival of Buncombe.* Baltimore: Johns Hopkins University Press, 1996 [1956].

Miller, Nathan. *New World Coming: The 1920s and the Making of Modern America.* New York: Scribner, 2003.

Nicolson, Harold. *Dwight Morrow.* New York: Harcourt, Brace, 1935.

Olasky, Marvin, and John Perry. *Monkey Business: The True Story of the Scopes Trial.* Nashville: Broadman & Holman, 2005.

Olney, Martha. *Buy Now, Pay Later: Advertising, Credit, and Consumer Durables in the 1920s.* Chapel Hill: University of North Carolina Press, 1991.

O'Reilly, Kenneth. *Nixon's Piano: Presidents and Racial Politics from Washington to Clinton.* New York: Free Press, 1995.

Orton, Vrest. *Calvin Coolidge's Unique Vermont Inauguration.* Rutland, VT: Academy Books, 1970.

Parrish, Michael. *Anxious Decades: America in Prosperity and Depression, 1920–1941.* New York: W. W. Norton, 1994.

Ponder, Stephen. *Managing the Press: Origins of the Media Presidency, 1897–1933.* New York: St. Martin's Press, 1999.

Ratner, Sidney. *Taxation and Democracy in America.* New York: John Wiley, 1967 [1942].

Rees, Matthew. *From the Deck to the Sea: Blacks and the Republican Party.* Wakefield, NH: Longwood Academic, 1991.

Russell, Francis. *A City in Terror: Calvin Coolidge and the 1919 Boston Police Strike.* Boston: Beacon Press, 1975.

Schlesinger, Arthur, Jr. *The Crisis of the Old Order, 1919–1933.* Boston: Houghton Mifflin, 1956.

Schlesinger, Arthur, Jr., and Fred L. Israel, eds. *History of American Presidential Elections, 1789–1968.* Vol. 6. New York: Chelsea House, 1985.

Silver, Thomas. *Coolidge and the Historians.* Durham, NC: Carolina Academic Press for the Claremont Institute, 1982.

Sobel, Robert. *Coolidge: An American Enigma.* Washington, DC: Regnery, 1998.

Soule, George. *Prosperity Decade: From War to Depression, 1917–1929.* White Plains, NY: M. E. Sharpe, 1975 [1947].

Sussman, Warren. *Culture as History: The Transformation of American Society in the Twentieth Century.* New York: Pantheon, 1984.

Tebbel, John, and Sarah Miles Watts. *The Press and the Presidency: From George Washington to Ronald Reagan.* New York: Oxford University Press, 1985.

Troy, Gil. *See How They Ran: The Changing Role of the Presidential Candidate.* Revised and expanded edition. Cambridge, MA: Harvard University Press, 1996 [1991].

Tulis, Jeffrey. *The Rhetorical Presidency.* Princeton, NJ: Princeton University Press, 1987.

Tye, Larry. *The Father of Spin: Edward L. Bernays and the Birth of Public Relations.* New York: Henry Holt, 1998.

Vickers, Raymond. *Panic in Paradise: Florida's Banking Crash of 1926.* Tuscaloosa: University of Alabama Press, 1994.

Wanniski Jude. *The Way the World Works.* Washington, DC: Regnery, 1998 [1978].

Watts, Steven. *The People's Tycoon: Henry Ford and the American Century.* New York: Alfred A. Knopf, 2005.

West, Nathanael. *Novels and Other Writings.* New York: Library of America, 1997.

Wheeler, Mark, ed. *The Economics of the Great Depression.* Kalamazoo, MI: W. E. Upjohn Institute for Employment Research, 1998.

White, William Allen. *A Puritan in Babylon: The Story of Calvin Coolidge.* Norwalk, CT: Easton Press, 1986 [1938].

ARTICLES: PRIMARY SOURCES

The Nation
The New Republic
The New York Times

Barton, Bruce. "Calvin Coolidge as Seen Through the Eyes of His Friends." *American Review of Reviews,* September 1923.

———. "Concerning Calvin Coolidge." *Collier's,* November 22, 1919.

———. "The Silent Man on Beacon Hill." *Women's Home Companion,* March 1920.

Bernays, Edward. "Manipulating Public Opinion: The Why and the How." *American Journal of Sociology* 33, no. 6 (May 1928).

Bliven, Bruce. "The Great Coolidge Mystery." *Harper's Monthly,* December 1925.

Bullard, F. Lauriston. "Calvin Coolidge as Man and Statesman." *Current History*, September 1923.

"Calvin Coolidge, American." *Outlook*, November 12, 1919.

Good Housekeeping, February 1935 and March 1935.

Lawrence, David. "President and Press." *Saturday Evening Post*, August 28, 1927.

Macdonald, William. "'Coolidge Prosperity' a Campaign Issue." *Current History*, November 1926.

New England Journal of History 55, no. 1 (Fall 1998).

Ratcliffe, S. K. "President Coolidge's Triumph." *Contemporary Review*, July 1924.

Rogers, Lindsay. "The White House Spokesman." *Virginia Quarterly Review*, July 1926.

Sanders, Everett. "Calvin Coolidge: A Profile." *Saturday Evening Post*, December 6, 1930.

Sharp, William. "President and Press." *Atlantic Monthly*, August 1927.

Shepherd, William. "The White House Says." *Collier's*, February 2, 1929.

"Three Men Who Work for Coolidge." *Literary Digest*, January 24, 1924.

ARTICLES: SECONDARY SOURCES

Alldredge, Everett. "Centennial History of First Congregational Church 1865–1965," available at http://www.fccuccdc.org/history.htm.

Berkman, Dave. "Politics and Radio in the 1924 Campaign." *Journalism Quarterly* 64, no. 2 (Summer/Fall 1987).

Blair, John. "Coolidge the Image-Maker: The President and the Press, 1923–1929." *New England Quarterly* 46, no. 4 (December 1973).

———. "A Time for Parting: The Negro During the Coolidge Years." *American Studies* 3, no. 2 (December 1969).

Buckley, W. Kerry. "A President for the 'Great Silent Majority': Bruce Barton's Construction of Calvin Coolidge." *New England Quarterly* 76, no. 4 (December 2003).

Cornwell, Elmer. "Coolidge and Presidential Leadership." *Public Opinion Quarterly* 21, no. 2 (Summer 1957).

Dailey, Maceo Crenshaw, Jr. "Calvin Coolidge's Afro-American Connection." *Contributions in Black Studies* 8 (1986–87).

Fenno, Richard. "Coolidge: Representative of the People." *Current History* 39, no. 230 (October 1960).

Fowler, Russell. "Calvin Coolidge and the Supreme Court." *Journal of Supreme Court History* 25, no. 3 (November 2000).

Glad, Paul. "Progressives and the Business Culture of the 1920s." *Journal of American History* 33, no. 1 (June 1966).

Henretta, James. "Charles Evans Hughes and the Strange Death of Liberal America." *Law and History Review* 24, no. 1 (Spring 2006).

Hynes, Terry. "Media Manipulation and Political Campaigns: Bruce Barton and the Presidential Elections of the Jazz Age." *Journalism History* 4, no. 3 (Autumn 1977).

Kane, Richard. "The Federal Segregation of Blacks During the Presidential Administrations of Warren G. Harding and Calvin Coolidge." *Pan-African Journal* 7, no. 2 (Summer 1974).

Maddox, Robert James. "Keeping Cool with Coolidge." *Journal of American History* 53, no. 4 (March 1967).

Marx, Fritz Morstein. "The Bureau of the Budget: Its Evolution and Present Role, I." *American Political Science Review* 39, no. 4 (August 1945).

Pearcy, Matthew. "After the Flood: A History of the 1928 Flood Control Act." *Journal of the Illinois State Historical Society* (Summer 2002).

Platt, Michael. "The Life of Calvin Coolidge." *Modern Age* 36, no. 4 (Summer 1994).

"The Racial Views of American Presidents: A Look at the Record of Calvin Coolidge." *Journal of Blacks in Higher Education* 21 (Autumn 1998).

Ribuffo, Leo. "Jesus Christ as Business Statesman: Bruce Barton and the Selling of Corporate Capitalism." *American Quarterly* 33, no. 2 (Summer 1981).

Sherman, Richard. "Republicans and Negroes: The Lessons of Normalcy." *Phylon* 27, no. 1 (1966).

Shogan, Colleen. "Coolidge and Reagan: The Rhetorical Influence of Silent Cal on the Great Communicator." *Rhetoric & Public Affairs* 9, no. 2 (Summer 2006).

Silver, Thomas. "Coolidge and the Historians." *American Scholar* 50, no. 4 (Autumn 1981).

Smiley, Gene, and Richard Keehn. "Federal Personal Income Tax Policy in the 1920s." *Journal of Economic History* 55, no. 2 (June 1995).

Ward, John. "The Meaning of Lindbergh's Flight." *American Quarterly* 10, no. 1 (Spring 1958).

Acknowledgments

Many people helped me in the writing of *Calvin Coolidge*, and I would like to thank them briefly here. At Times Books, Paul Golob first expressed interest in having me write for this series. He offered enthusiasm for the project and excellent advice throughout—and, lest I forget, edited the manuscript brilliantly. Also at Times Books, David Wallace-Wells ably assisted with a variety of tasks, always with good cheer—no surprise, given his *Slate* pedigree. Thanks to Chris O'Connell for overseeing the production editing as well. Once again, I am indebted to Peter Matson, agent par excellence, for his steady guiding hand, as well as to his talented assistants at Sterling Lord Literistic.

America has no greater historian than Arthur M. Schlesinger Jr. I was honored to receive his invitation to write for this series, and doubly honored to benefit from his perspicacious comments on a manuscript draft. If the privilege of his interest weren't enough, I was also fortunate to have another of America's most eminent historians and experts on the 1920s, William Leuchtenburg, read and comment on a draft. The final version profited immensely from his careful edits, down to suggestions about sentence structure. Warren Bass, Christopher Capozzola, Jim Cooke, Robert Greenberg, Andrew Jewett, Kevin C. Murphy, and Sheldon Stern all read manuscript drafts and offered valuable comments. I thank them for sharing their time, energy, and knowledge of history. Sheldon, who ran an important conference on Coolidge at the John F. Kennedy Presidential Library in 1998, offered helpful advice throughout the process. David Shreve, a superb historian of political economy, read the chapters on Coolidge's economics, saved me from many errors, and generously sent me articles and citations.

I very much appreciate the assorted favors, large and small, rendered by Alan Brinkley, Jonathan Chait, Gus Friedrich, David Kennedy, Yehuda Mirsky, John Pavlik, Steven Ponder, Matt Rees, Colleen Shogan, Linda Steiner, Steve Weisman, and Eric Yellin. I have probably omitted others who helped me; I thank them not only for their help but also for forgiving my lapses.

My thanks, too, to the archivists at the Library of Congress for their assistance, and to the White House Historical Association, the Rutgers University Office of Research and Sponsored Programs, and the Rutgers Initiative in the Interdisciplinary Study of Issues in Privacy and Security for funds that helped defray research expenses. The Aresty Center at Rutgers gave me the chance to benefit from Prudence Cho's excellent research assistance. I thank David Noyola, Kate Sell, and Dan Su for their indispensable research help as well.

My family, as always, provided much-appreciated support, ideas, and encouragement—thanks, Mom and Dad, Judith and Ira, Jon and Megan, and Renee. Suzanne's love, support, and companionship were critical in helping me get to the finish line. Most of all, I'm grateful to Leo for those times he came into my office, said, "Daddy working," and figured out that he should leave the room—and even more grateful for those times that he insisted I leave with him.

Index

ABOUT THE AUTHOR

———

DAVID GREENBERG is a professor of history and media studies at Rutgers University, a columnist for *Slate*, and the author of the prizewinning *Nixon's Shadow: The History of an Image*. A former acting editor of *The New Republic*, he has written for scholarly and popular publications including *The Atlantic Monthly*, *Foreign Affairs*, *The New York Times*, and *The Washington Post*. He lives in New York City.